The differences between a man and a woman are at the best so obstinate and exasperating that they practically cannot be got over unless there is an atmosphere of exaggerated tenderness and mutual interest.

G. K. CHESTERTON

Let marriage be held in honor among all.

Heb. 13:4 ESV

What a great idea to unearth wisdom from the past for life in the present. Who knew that people long gone with such unpronounceable names would live on in these lessons on marriage. This is historical theology at its best. Biblical, practical, wonderfully helpful and really enjoyable.

ALISTAIR BEGG,
Senior Pastor, Parkside Church, Chagrin Falls, Ohio

Christians have always honored marriage and understood it not only as a tremendous blessing instituted by the Creator Himself, but as a living picture of the relationship between Christ and his church. I am very thankful to Rob Plummer and Matt Haste for scouring Christianity's rich theological heritage and creating this compendium of reflections on marriage from Christian history's foremost pastors and theologians. *Held in Honor* is a wonderful, short resource for Christians as they seek to live out their marriages in a way that glorifies God and exalts the Gospel.

R. ALBERT MOHLER, JR.,
President, The Southern Baptist Theological Seminary, Louisville, Kentucky

As a woman who recently married for the first time at the age of 57 and who loves classic Christian writings and devotional literature, I have found this book to be a treasure trove. A sweet and timely source of wisdom as I seek to honor Christ in a new season and station of life.

NANCY DEMOSS WOLGEMUTH,
Author of *Revive Our Hearts*, radio host, Niles, Michigan

This inspiring collection of excerpts on marriage with accompanying devotionals will make stimulating reading for engaged and married couples and even singles. Based upon the premise that in our marriages we can learn from the wisdom of those before us, this volume gathers helpful advice from writers across the ages. Highly recommended!

ANDREAS J. KOSTENBERGER,
Founder of Biblical Foundations™
and co-author of *God, Marriage & Family* and *God's Design for Man & Woman*

What a delightful mix of historical wisdom, biblical truth, and real-world application. In these pages you'll hear the early church martyr Ignatius tell you "Marriage is God's good gift." Keep reading and you'll see how good and glorious of a gift it is.

STEPHEN J. NICHOLS,
President, Reformation Bible College, Sanford, Florida
Chief Academic Officer, Ligonier Ministries

Marriage, once deemed a relic of a bygone age, is suddenly back in fashion, albeit for many of the wrong reasons. This book offers a delightful survey of Christian thinking on the issue from ancient times to the present day. Theologically informative and instructive and yet devotional in approach, it makes a fine contribution to contemporary Christian reflection on a most important institution.

CARL R. TRUEMAN,
Paul Woolley Professor of Historical Theology and Church History,
Westminster Theological Seminary, Philadelphia, Pennsylvania

Good books on marriage are hard to find, but in *Held in Honor*, Robert Plummer and Matt Haste have taken an expedition through church history to bring back the finest gems of biblical teaching on marriage. Accompanied by biographical sketches and the authors' own commentary, this book will challenge, encourage, convict, and inspire every wife to cherish her marriage and prize her husband.

CAROLYN MAHANEY,
Author of *Feminine Appeal*, Blogger at www.girltalkhome.com

I do not know of a more interesting and scholarly book to recommend for a marriage-focused devotional. The wisdom is ancient, contemporary, and future like a wise father instructing his son before a white wedding. I am thankful for Robert Plummer and Matt Haste's careful and substantive work reclaiming these gems from throughout church history for our current devotion. I believe *Held in Honor* will both challenge the church to be wise in marriage and provoke the church to worship our God. Buy this book, treasure it on your nightstand, and don't forget to pass it to your sons and daughters as their marriage date approaches.

DANIEL MONTGOMERY,
Lead Pastor, Sojourn Community Church, Louisville, Kentucky
Founder of the Sojourn Network and author of *Faithmapping* and *PROOF*

Plummer and Haste's *Held in Honor: Wisdom for Your Marriage from Voices of the Past* is a collection of writings on marriage from Christian theologians, pastors, and authors. The work is a delight to read on many levels. Those who value church history will appreciate the profound reflections on marriage from some of the greatest Christian minds of the past. Those who seek to understand Scripture's teaching on marriage will be rewarded and those who wish to be challenged to live with greater devotion toward God and his or her spouse will find many practical insights. The authors present a realistic understanding of marriage, highlighting its joys and sorrows, as well as its triumphs and trials. I highly recommend this book.

MICHAEL L. BRYANT,
Dean, School of Christian Studies,
Charleston Southern University, Charleston, South Carolina

HELD IN
HONOR

Wisdom for Your Marriage
from Voices of the Past

Robert L. Plummer
& Matthew D. Haste

CHRISTIAN
FOCUS

Copyright © Robert L. Plummer and Matthew D. Haste, 2015

paperback ISBN 978-1-78191-643-8
epub ISBN 978-1-78191-690-2
mobi ISBN 978-1-78191-691-9

Published in 2015 and reprinted in 2016 with Truth For Life
by
Christian Focus Publications Ltd.
Geanies House, Fearn, Ross-shire,
IV20 1TW, Scotland, UK

www.christianfocus.com

Cover design by Pete Barnsley (CreativeHoot.com)

Printed in the U.S.A.

Contents

REFORMATION & PURITAN ERA (c. 1400–1700)

EARLY EVANGELICAL ERA (c. 1700–1900)

MODERN ERA (c. 1900–Present)

Acknowledgements

We are grateful to the many people who helped make this book possible. First, we thank our Triune God who, in His infinite wisdom, created marriage as a picture of Christ and His church. Second, sincere appreciation is due to Willie MacKenzie and Christian Focus Publications. Third, at the risk of forgetting a deserving co-laborer, we want to thank various research assistants and proofreaders: Robert Brandhagen, Rod Elledge, Tyler Flatt, Cheyenne Haste, John Lowe, Ryan Rice, Mark A. Seifrid, Bill Starr, Ryan West, Joel Wildberger, and Katherine Anne Wildberger. Thank you to the various publishers and authors who granted permission to use their work in this volume. All quoted materials are public domain or used with permission. Copies of publishers' permissions are on file with Christian Focus.

Finally, in a book about marriage, we would be remiss not to thank our wives and children for their support and sacrifice.

As husbands, we regularly fail to reflect clearly the perfect love of Jesus for His church, but we pray that God would graciously continue to shape us into the image of His Son.

So, it is to our beloved wives that we dedicate this book.

To Chandi Plummer and Cheyenne Haste

πισταὶ ἀδελφαὶ ἐν κυρίῳ

Introduction

In his classic work *Orthodoxy*, G. K. Chesterton tells a story about an English yachtsman who discovered an island after drifting off his course, only to realize that this exciting new land was in fact the other side of England. Chesterton employs the image to poke fun at himself, admitting that in his youth he sought every attempt to uncover his own truths, only to find that others had long since reached the same conclusions. Humbly, Chesterton admits, "I am the man who with the utmost daring discovered what had been discovered before." His humorous story of a man bent on charting his own course merely to land where countless others had gone before is a helpful place to begin this little book on marriage. What Chesterton confessed about his worldview, others are guilty of trying in their marriages.

Many approach marriage as if it were an adventure into the unknown. It is surely an adventure, but it does not have to be as perilous as some make it to be. God has intended marriage to be a blessing received with gratitude (1 Tim. 4:3-4), yet for many, it can feel like a summons to a strange and distant land. As you pick up this book, you may find yourself in some deep waters that are wholly unfamiliar to you. Perhaps you are engaged to be married and beginning to look out at the horizon of lifetime commitment that awaits you. Or maybe you have been married for many years and feel like your marriage is beginning to crash upon the rocks. You might be single and simply interested in exploring something you hope to experience someday. For all of us, marriage can be a bit intimidating. We are commanded to hold it in honor (Heb. 13:4), yet many of us approach it with fear.

Both Chesterton and the yachtsman from his story eventually found themselves in pleasant places (one spiritually, the other geographically). Their warning to us is not to avoid their conclusions but rather to learn from their misguided beginnings. Each of their failures was rooted in a refusal to consult the wisdom of others. The lesson regarding marriage should be clear: If we are to honor God in our homes, we must look outside of ourselves to those who have sailed these waters before us.

This book aims to be a guide to anyone interested in applying that bit of wisdom to their own marriage. It is built on a few foundational convictions. First, when you walk down the aisle, you are treading an ancient path. There is, after all, nothing new under the sun (Eccles. 1:9), and that includes the challenges you are facing (or might someday meet) in your marriage. Second, the Lord has graciously provided beacons in the darkness. There are guides who have gone before you and have wisdom to share. God has continually raised up and gifted teachers for His church (Eph. 4:11-12). How foolish it would be to ignore them! Third, there is but one True Light by which you may safely chart your course. Marriage was created by God (Gen. 2:24), it is enacted by God (Matt. 19:6), and therefore, God Himself must have the final word on what it should look like (e.g., Eph. 5:22-33). All marriages find their ultimate meaning in the spiritual union of Christ and His church. The voices in this book are only as useful as they serve to point you to that reality.

Although the union of a man and a woman in matrimony may look different in any given time or place, there are common challenges that transcend culture, age, ethnicity, and context. This devotional seeks to invite you into that common experience by pointing you to the wisdom of the past. Are you single and wondering how to meet the right person? Consider the example of George Whitefield and his prayer that God would provide him a wife as you wait patiently on the Lord. Are you newly married and struggling to find your way as a couple? Be encouraged by Elisabeth Elliot's candid description of the realities that all couples face after the honeymoon. Perhaps you are a husband feeling overwhelmed by your responsibilities as a leader? Let the words of Matthew Henry guide you toward walking with integrity in your home. Are you a wife burdened by the challenges of respecting your unkind husband? Listen to how Augustine described the faithfulness of his mother, Monica, and the impact it had on her harsh partner. Maybe this book is a final effort by some pastor or counselor to help heal a marriage that seems broken beyond repair. May the words of Martyn Lloyd-Jones remind us all that in our marriages, we have put more than just our own reputations on the line. The very name of God and the integrity of His gospel hang in the balance as couples live out each day of their lives together.

Regardless of where you are in the journey of marriage, we can all benefit from hearing from others along the way. We don't want to be like Chesterton or his poor yachtsman—too ashamed to ask for help and too foolish to listen to others. Marriage was never meant to be a lonely voyage. The Lord has provided a great cloud of witnesses who can speak to its joys and strengthen you in its trials. The men and women quoted in this book provide a collection of uniquely Christian reflections on the subject with the aim that marriage might be, in the words of the author of Hebrews, "held in honor by all" (Heb. 13:4). We pray that the pages ahead encourage you toward faithfulness and bring glory to God, who loves His people so extravagantly that He calls them His Bride (Rev. 21:9).

PATRISTIC ERA

(c. 100–500)

Love Your Wife

IGNATIUS OF ANTIOCH (D. 107)

Ignatius of Antioch, a first-century bishop mentored in the faith by the Apostle John, lived during a time of great persecution. Despite the hostility around him, Ignatius faithfully pastored his congregation for over forty years before he was sentenced to death. As he journeyed to Rome for his execution, he penned several letters to Christians throughout the empire, encouraging them in the faith and combating doctrinal errors. While addressing various concerns of the early church, Ignatius took time to encourage husbands and wives to honor God in their marriages.

Beloved Bishop Polycarp, do not simply resist—but literally *run away* from dark and wicked things. Speak clearly and publicly about these matters. Regarding the women in your Christian gatherings—teach them to be satisfied not only physically with their husbands, but also to strive for an inner spiritual contentment. Likewise, as you minister in the name of Jesus Christ, instruct the men to love their wives as Christ himself loved the church.

If God has gifted some among your congregations to remain unmarried, celibate and devoted to the Lord's work—such a sacrifice is to be done without fanfare. This calling is for the honor of God! Boasting about such matters reveals a diseased spiritual condition. You can be sure that such arrogant "super spiritual" people will end up criticizing you and other church leaders, Polycarp. Watch out! There will be no end to their self-promotion.

Don't be deceived! Marriage is God's good gift to men and women. And, as bishop, you have the joyful task of celebrating and honoring marriage in your community. Encourage husbands and wives not to enter marriage simply as a means of satisfying their sexual appetites, but with a consciousness of God's command to love and sacrifice for each other. Each marriage is ultimately for the honor of God.

≈≈≈

Ignatius, *Letter to Polycarp* 5.1–2
Paraphrastic translation by Robert L. Plummer.

DEVOTION

In the modern world, our lives are quite fragmented. Men and women spend more hours per day with co-workers than with their own spouses. This situation can be especially dangerous if a person is not emotionally and sexually satisfied with his or her spouse.

Ignatius tells Polycarp to encourage Christian women to "be satisfied not only physically with their husbands, but also to strive for an inner spiritual contentment." Christian men are not to take their wives for granted, but to love them deliberately in the pattern of Christ's sacrificial love (Eph. 5:21-33).

How can you find satisfaction in a spouse who is frequently unsatisfying? In such a situation, you must remember that every marriage is between two sinners who can never ultimately satisfy each other. Your deepest longings for meaning and belonging can only be found in relationship with Christ. With Christ at the center of your life, however, you can reach out in love and service to the undeserving. God can change your selfish heart, so that you no longer ask "What has my wife/husband done for me lately?" but "What can I do to serve my spouse?" Empowered by the Holy Spirit, you will find it is truly "more blessed to give than to receive" (Acts 20:35).

One explicit command in Scripture (alluded to by Ignatius) is not to deny your spouse regular God-honoring sexual relations (1 Cor 7:3-7). By meeting your spouse's needs (sexual, emotional, or spiritual), you help place a fence of protection around your marriage. Read 1 Corinthians 7:3-5 and ask God how you are doing with fulfilling the Apostle Paul's instructions in your own marriage.

Surviving a Bad Marriage

JUSTIN MARTYR (100–165)

Justin Martyr was the most significant Christian apologist of the second century. Having converted to Christianity after years of searching for truth through Greek philosophy, Justin became an ardent defender of the faith—a ministry which eventually cost him his life. In the following excerpt, Justin tells the story of a Christian woman in a difficult marriage to an unbeliever. His description of her situation reveals many of the challenges that Christians faced in second-century Rome as well as the church's resolve to remain faithful to God despite their circumstances.

A certain woman lived with a drunkard husband; she herself was formerly a heavy drinker as well. But when she came to the knowledge of the teachings of Christ she became sober-minded, and sought to persuade her husband likewise to repent of his wild living, citing the teaching of Christ, and assuring him that there would be punishment in eternal fire inflicted upon those who do not turn away from sin and follow the Lord in holiness. But he would not listen to her and plunged further into sin, deeply hurting his wife. The godly woman considered divorcing him, for in truth, her husband was bound not to her—but to his wicked, unlawful passions. Yet, with the strength of Christian friends around her, she resolved to continue to love him in hopes that he might be won over to Christ.

Justin Martyr, *The Second Apology of Justin for the Christians Addressed to the Roman Senate*, Ante-Nicene Fathers, ed. Philip Schaff and Henry Wace (Peabody, MA: Hendricksons, 1885; repr., 2004), 1:188.
[Language Updated]

DEVOTION

Justin Martyr understood that our behavior reveals who we really are. We are constantly giving external evidence of our inner spiritual condition.

The Apostle Paul touches on this same subject in Galatians 5:19-21. He writes, "Now the works of the flesh are evident: sexual immorality, impurity, sensuality, idolatry, sorcery, enmity, strife, jealousy, fits of anger, rivalries, dissensions, divisions, envy, drunkenness, orgies, and things like these. I warn you, as I warned you before, that those who do such things will not inherit the kingdom of God."

While the Bible teaches that salvation is an undeserved gift from God (Rom. 3:23-24), it also teaches that a person who has been saved will demonstrate that new reality in their lives. One cannot be in genuine relationship with a holy, loving God without experiencing an ongoing transformation of love and holiness in their lives.

Can you imagine someone getting up to give their testimony and saying, "I was a drunk and into witchcraft before I was saved by Jesus. And, well, now I'm saved, and I'm still a drunk and into witchcraft." That's not a testimony; it's near blasphemy! As one theologian has said, "Faith alone saves, but faith that saves is never alone, but is always accompanied by fruit that shows the reality of that faith."

How is your marriage different because you are a Christian? What transforming evidences of God's Spirit are visible in the way you relate to your spouse? Ask God to lay bare your soul before Him. If there are no genuine evidences of grace in your married life, is it possible that you do not know God?

If this is the case, do not despair, but receive this invitation from Jesus:

Come to me, all who labor and are heavy laden, and I will give you rest. Take my yoke upon you, and learn from me, for I am gentle and lowly in heart, and you will find rest for your souls. For my yoke is easy, and my burden is light (Matt. 11:28-30).

Guard Your Mind

THE SHEPHERD OF HERMAS (C.150)

Although little is known about its author, *The Shepherd of Hermas* was a popular work in the early church. Believed to have been written in Rome around the middle of the second century, it contains a record of several visits from an angel, or shepherd, to a man named Hermas. The angel's message focuses on the failings of the church at the time and the need for repentance. In addition, the angel gives Hermas twelve mandates for holy living, including the following advice about pursuing purity in mind and heart.

Then the angelic messenger said to me, "I solemnly charge you to be a man of complete sexual purity. Bar the door of your mind—keep out every lustful thought! Be on guard against any form of sexual impurity or perversion. Do you not realize that when you entertain a lustful thought, you are committing a great sin? Instead of lusting after other women, you should focus your thoughts on your wife. If you do this, you will stay on the straight path of purity.

"If, however, you allow lustful thoughts to flit through your mind, you can be sure that you are walking down a sinful path. Don't you realize that entertaining sexual thoughts about any woman other than your wife is greatly displeasing to God? How can a servant of God also be a slave to sin? If you play with lust, you are jumping over a steep cliff towards eternal death!

"Watch out! I can't say this enough—stay far away from the edge of lust's cliff. Dear man, God has saved you to live a righteous life. Beloved servant, God has rescued you for a life of purity. Stay away from every impure thought!"

❦

The Shepherd of Hermas, Mandate 4, 1:1-3
Paraphrastic translation by Robert L. Plummer.

DEVOTION

"It's OK to look as long as you don't touch." Thus are the sexual ethics of a fallen world filled with provocative images and scantily-clad persons. *The Shepherd of Hermas*, on the other hand, points us to a biblical understanding of sexuality. The angel says, "Bar the door of your mind— keep out every lustful thought! Be on guard against any form of sexual impurity or perversion. Do you not realize that when you entertain a lustful thought, you are committing a great sin?"

Jesus used similar language in the Sermon on the Mount, saying, "You have heard that it was said, 'You shall not commit adultery.' But I say to you that everyone who looks at a woman with lustful intent has already committed adultery with her in his heart. If your right eye causes you to sin, tear it out and throw it away. For it is better that you lose one of your members than that your whole body be thrown into hell. And if your right hand causes you to sin, cut it off and throw it away. For it is better that you lose one of your members than that your whole body go into hell" (Matt. 5:27-30).

Unfaithfulness to your spouse does not begin in another person's bedroom, but in your mind. Entertaining sexual thoughts about someone other than your spouse is adultery in the eyes of God, and over time, will lead to physical acts of adultery. Read through Matthew 5:27-30. Ask God, "Where have I been an adulterer/adulteress in thought or deed? Where have my eyes or mind lingered so as to dishonor you or my spouse?" Also ask yourself, "Am I dressing or acting in such a way to tempt others to adulterous thoughts?" Share your failures or temptations with another trusted Christian (James 5:16). Praise God that He accepts you through the perfect life and atoning death of Christ.

How Beautiful the Marriage of Two Christians

TERTULLIAN (160–220)

Tertullian was one of the most significant theologians of the early church. From his native Carthage, he vigorously defended the faith through influential writings such as his *Apology, Against Marcion*, and *The Prescription of Heretics*. Although trained as a lawyer, his reflections on the Trinity significantly impacted the theological discussions of his day. Despite his involvement with a legalistic offshoot of Christianity known as Montanism in his later years, he provided one of the most memorable quotes about marriage from the ancient world.

How beautiful, then, the marriage of two Christians, two who are one in hope, one in desire, one in the way of life they follow, one in the religion they practice. They are as brother and sister, both servants of the same Master. Nothing divides them, either in flesh or in spirit. They are, in very truth, *two in one flesh*; and where there is but one flesh there is also but one spirit. They pray together, they worship together, they fast together; instructing one another, encouraging one another, strengthening one another. Side by side they visit God's church and partake of God's Banquet; side by side they face difficulties and persecution, share their consolations. They have no secrets from one another; they never shun each other's company; they never bring sorrow to each other's hearts. Unembarrassed, they visit the sick and assist the needy. They give alms without anxiety; they attend the Sacrifice without difficulty; they perform their daily exercises of piety without hindrance … Psalms and hymns they sing to one another, striving to see which one of them will chant more beautifully the praises of their Lord. Hearing and seeing this, Christ rejoices. To such as these He gives His peace. *Where there are two together*, there also He is present; and where He is, there evil is not.

❧❧❧

Tertullian, *To His Wife* 4.2.8 in *Tertullian. Treatises on Marriage and Remarriage*, trans. William P. Le Saint, Ancient Christian Writers, ed. Johannes Quasten and Joseph C. Plumpe (Westminster, MD: The Newman Press, 1951), 35–36.

DEVOTION

Tertullian's poetic description above reminds us that we are right to turn people's eyes to the beauty of marriage—for the institution reflects the goodness of the God who created it. Marriage can serve as a God-glorifying theological primer for many lessons. Let us consider briefly two of these.

First, the wedding itself illustrates the power of God's creative word. In Genesis, we read that God spoke into nothing, and the universe sprang into existence (Gen. 1:1-27). Through the word of the gospel, new life springs into the hearts of former rebels. "So faith comes from hearing, and hearing through the word of Christ" (Rom. 10:17). At a wedding, the bride and groom speak words of commitment to one another. And, as the pastor says, "I now pronounce you man and wife," a new legal and relational reality comes into existence.

Second, a marriage mirrors both the legal and loving aspects of God's covenant relationship with His people. Where else in modern society do legality and love meet? A marriage is a formal and solemn agreement, but it is an agreement entered into with joy, expectation, and emotional commitment. A marriage is a *covenant*, but even that word, in its watered-down secular usage, does not do justice to the permanence of the marriage relationship.

Reflect on how the covenant of marriage can help you understand the New Covenant that God has instituted with His people through the death of Christ. Hundreds of years prior to the coming of Christ, God spoke of this New Covenant through the prophet Jeremiah:

> For this is the covenant that I will make with the house of Israel after those days, declares the LORD: I will put my law within them, and I will write it on their hearts. And I will be their God, and they shall be my people. And no longer shall each one teach his neighbor and each his brother, saying, "Know the LORD," for they shall all know me, from the least of them to the greatest, declares the LORD. For I will forgive their iniquity, and I will remember their sin no more (Jer. 31:33-34).

Does the way you think of or speak about your husband or wife reflect the covenantal nature of your relationship? Do you recognize the binding legal and loving aspects of your marriage? If someone observed your marriage, what would they conclude about God and His covenant love? Perhaps today you can remind your spouse that you treasure him or her as your lifelong covenant partner. Whatever challenges you face, thank God for His wisdom in bringing the two of you together.

The Beauty of Purity

THE CLEMENTINE HOMILIES (c. 250)

The Clementine Homilies are a collection of fictitious stories about the disciples of Christ that provide an interesting window into the theology of the early church. Although the author and date of this work are unclear, scholars generally believe it was composed in the third century and later attributed to Clement. Despite the inexact details of its genesis, *The Clementine Homilies* remain a valuable resource for understanding what some early Christians believed. In the following quotation, the author reveals his appreciation of a woman who practices purity and describes her godliness in glowing terms.

The pure woman longs for God, loves God, pleases God, glorifies God; and to men she affords no occasion for slander. The pure woman perfumes the Church with her good reputation, and glorifies it by her piety. She is, moreover, the praise of her teachers, and a helper to them in their purity.

The pure woman is adorned with the Son of God as with a bridegroom. She is clothed with holy light. Her beauty lies in a well-regulated soul; and she is fragrant with ointment, even with a good reputation. She is arrayed in beautiful clothing, even in modesty. She wears about her precious pearls, even pure words. And she is radiant, for her mind has been brilliantly lighted up. Onto a beautiful mirror does she look, for she looks into God. Beautiful cosmetics does she use, namely, the fear of God, with which she admonishes her soul. Beautiful is the woman not because she has chains of gold on her, but because she has been set free from passing worldly lusts. The pure woman is greatly desired by the great King; she has been wooed, watched, and loved by Him. The pure woman does not parade her beauty or shapeliness before strangers – but only to her own husband. The pure woman is grieved to discover that her behavior or dress has tempted a man to lust after her.

⁓⁓

"Homily 13, Chapter 15-16," in *The Clementine Homilies*, Ante-Nicene Fathers, ed. Alexander Roberts and James Donaldson (Peabody, MA: Hendrickson, 1886; repr., 2004), 8:303.

DEVOTION

A careful reading of the above quote in its broader context reveals that the author of *The Clementine Homilies* has in mind an unmarried woman who lives a virgin life—wholly consecrated to the bridegroom of Christ. Yet, the concern for the way a woman's behavior and dress affect others is timeless wisdom.

In their book *Girl Talk*, Carolyn Mahaney and Nicole Whitacre state bluntly of fallen humanity, "Guys lust and girls want to be lusted after." The sinful world encourages women to present themselves seductively with low necklines and tight clothes.

Yes, godly woman, it *will* cost you more time and money to find suitable clothes that are not seductive. But God wants you to present yourself as a human to be valued, not a sexual object to be consumed. And your Christian brothers will be most grateful for helping them to view you as a "sister in absolute purity" (1 Tim. 5:2).

Sexual dress and behavior are not sinful, of course, when expressed privately in the covenant relationship of marriage. Read the Song of Solomon!

Charming speech and a beautiful face are also gifts from a gracious God—gifts that we note He distributes, according to His common grace, among all peoples of the world. There are hundreds of millions of attractive, charming non-Christian women found all over the world—which is God's common grace to them and to their husbands! Sadly, outward charm and external beauty may mask a wicked heart.

A greater beauty—a lasting and eternal beauty—is found in the inner life of the woman who knows and fears God. As the author of Proverbs says, "Charm is deceptive, and beauty is fleeting; but a woman who fears the LORD is to be praised" (Prov. 31:30 NIV).

Wife, do you have an enduring, lasting, inner beauty which comes from knowing God and living in submission to Him? What do you spend more time cultivating: your outer beauty or your inner beauty?

Single woman, are you living in purity as you wait on the Lord to bring you a godly husband? Are you seeking to guard your Christian brothers from lust?

Husband, do you show your wife that your affection is bound fast by her inner beauty that will only shine brighter as her outward beauty fades?

Single man, as you seek a godly spouse, do you give most attention to the lasting beauty of a woman's inner life?

Marriage and Virginity

ATHANASIUS (296–373)

Athanasius was the bishop of Alexandria for over four decades, even though he was exiled from his post numerous times. Known as "the Father of Orthodoxy," Athanasius fought for a biblically faithful understanding of the Trinity, especially in relation to the deity of Christ. In the quote below, he answers his opponents as he did on other issues, by appealing to biblical truth. Nevertheless, his commitment to the Scriptures did not protect him from all misinterpretations, as the quote below illustrates. Like many in his day, Athanasius underappreciated marriage in his efforts to exalt the blessedness of celibacy.

For there are two ways in life, as touching these matters. The one the more moderate and ordinary, I mean marriage; the other angelic and unsurpassed, namely virginity. Now if a man chooses the way of the world, namely marriage, he is not indeed to blame; yet he will not receive such great gifts as the other. For he will receive, since he too brings forth fruit, namely thirtyfold. But if a man embrace the holy and unearthly way, even though, as compared with the former, it be rugged and hard to accomplish, yet it has the more wonderful gifts: for it grows the perfect fruit, namely an hundredfold

〜〜〜

Athanasius, "Letter XLVIII: Letter to Amun," in *Athanasius: Select Works and Letters*, Nicene and Post-Nicene Fathers, ed. Philip Schaff and Henry Wace (Peabody, MA: Hendrickson, 1892; repr., 2004), 4:556-57.

DEVOTION

Numerous writers in the early church deviated from the Scriptures in promoting life-long celibacy. Undoubtedly, remaining unmarried allows one to serve God with fewer distractions (1 Cor. 7:32-35), but such a life requires the supernatural gift of God and should not be viewed as the norm (1 Cor. 7:7). The Bible celebrates marriage as a gift of God for the majority of people (1 Cor. 7:2).

In the quote above, Athanasius values celibacy too highly by comparing it to the hundredfold fruit in Jesus' Parable of the Sower (Mark 4:8), while saying that the married Christian only bears thirtyfold.

In the twenty-first century in which we live, where has the church's view of marriage deviated from the Scriptures? If Jesus delays His return, where will future generations of Christians look back and shake their heads in disapproval?

The current prevalence of divorce among God's people will likely shock future generations of Christians. Malachi 2:16 warns: "'For I hate divorce!' says the LORD, the God of Israel. 'To divorce your wife is to overwhelm her with cruelty,' says the LORD of Heaven's Armies. 'So guard your heart; do not be unfaithful to your wife.'" (NLT)

Although the Scriptures seem to make allowance for divorce in the cases of adultery or abandonment (Matt. 5:32; 1 Cor. 7:15), too many professing Christians treat their marriages as mere relationships of convenience. When they grow weary of their current spouse, they move on.

Sociological research has shown that people who divorce because they are unhappy are generally even more unhappy five years down the road. Unhappy people who stay married, however, are generally happier five years in the future. Regardless of happiness, however, God's word calls a husband and wife to life-long faithfulness to the covenant of marriage. God hates divorce (Mal. 2:16).

If you are reading this devotional as a divorced person, do not despair. Even an unbiblical divorce is not a hopeless situation but a call to repent and receive the forgiveness of God.

Regardless of your past, if you are married now and were to grow deeply unhappy in your marriage, would you consider divorcing your spouse? Unless your answer is a resounding "No!" then you are not living in submission to God's Word.

Do Not Fight

JOHN CHRYSOSTOM (347–407)

John of Antioch was considered one of the greatest preachers of the early church, a fact commemorated in the name by which he is typically known: Chrysostom, the "golden-mouthed" one. John taught in his native Antioch for over ten years until he was kidnapped and forced to become the archbishop of Constantinople. In the capital city, he continued his preaching ministry until his golden mouth began to get him into trouble. He was eventually exiled as a heretic, but was exonerated after his death. The quote below illustrates John's passionate preaching and his concern for practical holiness.

Do not fight; for nothing is more bitter than this fighting, when it takes place on the part of the husband toward the wife. For the arguments that happen between beloved persons are bitter; and the Apostle shows that it arises from great bitterness, when, he says, anyone is at variance with his own members. To love therefore is the husband's part; to follow pertains to the wife. If then each one contributes his own part, all stands firm.

From being loved, the wife too becomes loving; and from her being submissive, the husband becomes yielding. See how in nature it has been so ordered, that the one should love and the other obey.

Do not therefore, husband, because your wife is subject to you, act like a despot; nor because your husband loves you should you as a wife be puffed up. Let neither the husband's love cause pride in the wife, nor the wife's respect puff up the husband. For this cause has God subjected her to you, O husband, that she may be loved all the more. For this cause He has made you to be loved, O wife, that you may more easily bear your role. Do not fear being a subject; for subjection to one that loves you has no hardship. Do not fear to love, for you have her respect. In no other way could your bond have been made. You have the authority of necessity, proceeding from nature; maintain also the bond that proceeds from love, for this allows the weaker to be endurable.

❧❧

John Chrysostom, "Homily 10," in *Homilies on Colossians*, Nicene & Post-Nicene Fathers (Peabody, MA: Hendrickson, 1889; repr., 2004), 13:304. [Language Updated]

DEVOTION

"Husbands, love your wives, and do not be harsh with them" (Col. 3:19).

From John Chrysostom's quote above, we see that harsh husbands and disrespectful wives are not the result of our modern culture, but evidence of the world's brokenness in every culture.

Let us not, however, leave this discussion in ethereal abstractions: Husband, do you speak more kindly to a potential business client than to your wife?

Don't deceive yourself. Your wife is not the problem. She does not deserve your harsh tone. Rather, your pride and greed are so strong that they enable you to mask your sin temporarily with outsiders. Truth be told, you prostitute your kindness for the money and respect of others. Your real identity is seen in those unguarded moments when you are tired, hungry, and inconvenienced in your own home. Your wife is still going to sleep with you and fix you supper, even if you were a little sharp with her, right? (Do you see how this skewed thinking reduces your wife to just another "supplier" to satisfy your demands?)

But, guilty sinner, do not despair. "The Lord is near" (Phil. 4:5b NIV). He is near in the sense that nothing you do is hidden from His sight, and He will hold you accountable for your secret sins. The Lord will defend your wife. The Lord is also near with grace, forgiveness and empowering to make you into a loving, gentle man. "Let your gentleness be evident to all" (Phil. 4:5a NIV).

Wife, you too should ask, "Have I shown my husband proper respect?" Is it possible that you are more respectful towards your children's teachers, your pastor, or your boss than towards your husband? Note the Bible says to respect your husband at all times—not only when he deserves it.

Married to a Merciless Man

AUGUSTINE OF HIPPO (354–430)

Few theologians can claim the legacy of Augustine of Hippo. In addition to pastoring his congregation, he wrote numerous treatises defending Christianity and set forth a theological system that continues to impact the church today. His most beloved work is *Confessions*, a spiritual autobiography praising God for his grace in Augustine's life. One of the most significant influences on Augustine was his mother, Monica, whose piety made a strong impression on her son and eventually won over her husband, Patrick, as well. In the excerpt below, Augustine described Monica's disposition toward her difficult husband and her commitment to pursuing peace in her home.

[Words addressed by Augustine to God about his godly mother.]

So she was brought up in modesty and sobriety. She was made by you [God] obedient to her parents rather than by them to you. When she reached marriageable age, she was given to a man and served him as her lord. She tried to win him for you, speaking to him of you by her virtues through which you made her beautiful, so that her husband loved, respected and admired her. She bore with his infidelities and never had any quarrel with her husband on this account. For she looked forward to your mercy coming upon him, in hope that, as he came to believe in you, he might become chaste. Furthermore, he was exceptional both for his kindness and for his quick temper. She knew that an angry husband should not be opposed, not merely by anything she did, nor even by a word. Once she saw that he had become calm and quiet, and that the occasion was opportune, she would explain the reason for her action, in case perhaps he had reacted without sufficient consideration.

~~~

Augustine, *Confessions*, Book IX.19, trans. Henry Chadwick (Oxford: University Press, 2009), 168-69. By permission of Oxford University Press.

DEVOTION

"For this is how the holy women who hoped in God used to adorn themselves, by submitting to their own husbands, as Sarah obeyed Abraham, calling him lord. And you are her children, if you do good and do not fear anything that is frightening" (1 Peter 3:5-6).

Television and movies tell women to make themselves beautiful by revealing their bodies, by adorning themselves with fancy clothes and expensive jewelry, and by flirting with men. The Bible says that godly women adorn themselves through their loving submission to their husbands. Women can be "children of Sarah" (showing their likeness to their "mother") if they live in the pattern of Abraham's wife. Augustine saw this beautiful pattern in his mother's life, and the quote above reminds us that a submissive, godly wife not only blesses her husband, but her children—and then through them, countless others.

If you are a woman, the Bible's teaching on submission can be hard to accept. "Listen, my husband is no Abraham!" you may say. On the other hand, Abraham tried to pass off his wife as his sister (Gen. 20:1-18), so maybe it's good that you are not married to him! And, certainly, Monica's husband sounds as bad as they come.

Every man in this broken world will sometimes waver in his faith and obedience. It seems a terribly frightening thing to sign up unconditionally, for a lifetime, to follow a man who is destined to disappoint. Yet, the grace and love you extend to your husband in his faltering leadership is a beautiful thing to him and to God—much more lasting and beautiful than an airbrushed photo on the cover of a magazine.

Perhaps you know someone who is married to a particularly difficult spouse. How can you pray for them today? How might he or she be encouraged by the example of Monica?

A Patristic Wedding Poem

PAULINUS OF NOLA (354–431)

Paulinus of Nola was an early Christian poet lauded for his rejection of wealth and embrace of the ascetic life. The following excerpt comes from a marriage poem he composed for the wedding of Julian of Eclanum (386-455), who famously sparred with Augustine on the issue of sexuality. The poem contrasts the Christian vision of marriage with the notions of Roman culture. In place of lavish pagan ceremonies, Paulinus called for simplicity that centered on God's purposes. Instead of outward adornment and expensive decor, he charged the bride and groom to cultivate the kind of modesty and piety that would honor the Lord.

Harmonious souls are being united in chaste love,
A youth who is Christ's virgin, a maiden who is God's.

Christ our God, lead to your reins these well-matched doves, and
Govern them under your easy yoke.

For your yoke, O Christ, is easy, when a ready will
Receives it, and love makes light the burden of obedience.

The sacred duty of chastity is a heavy weight for the unwilling,
But to the pious it is a sweet task to conquer the work of the
flesh …

For the harmonious bond of marriage shares at once in the
Love of piety, the dignity of love, and the peace of God.

With his own lips God made this union holy,
By the divine hand he established the human couple.

He made the two abide in one flesh,
In order to create a love more indivisible.

For while Adam slept the rib was snatched from him,
But soon he received his partner made from his own bone.

He experienced no harm, for his flesh was immediately replaced;
It was then that he realized a twin had been made from him.

When he saw that another had been formed out of him in the
union of their bodies,
He became a prophet of himself, speaking in a new voice.

This, he said, *is flesh of my flesh, I see here the bone of my bone.*
She is the rib from my side.

❦

Paulinus of Nola, "Carmen 25," in *Marriage in the Early Church*, trans. and ed. David G. Hunter (Minneapolis: Augsburg Fortress, 1992), 128-29.

DEVOTION

"Then the man said, 'This at last is bone of my bones and flesh of my flesh; she shall be called Woman, because she was taken out of Man'" (Gen. 2:23).

As Paulinus of Nola notes above, Adam greeted his wife with a joyful song, recognizing her as the perfect life partner for him. We can make a number of observations about this "first human song" in Genesis 2:23.

1. In the wisdom of God, Adam had not yet been provided with a life partner. For some unspecified period of time, Adam was aware of his aloneness in this beautiful new world. The man certainly had many thoughts and joyful tasks but no like-creature with whom to share them. God's timing and provision are always perfect. Perhaps an older single reader can be encouraged in remembering that truth.

2. Though God is not explicitly mentioned in this verse, He undergirds the passive construction, "she was taken." By whom was she taken out of Man? Certainly, none other than the Lord. As Paulinus says beautifully, "For while Adam slept the rib was snatched from him." Who did the snatching? God! A man can idolize his wife, but a joyful gratitude in God's provision of a wife is pleasing to the Lord. The lyrics of Genesis 2:23 are sung in a pre-Fall sinless state.

3. A healthy marriage should result in verbalizing your appreciation for your spouse. Christians should not mindlessly imitate the current chart-topping secular love songs. Nevertheless, though sinfully distorted, these songs rebuke the lack of spontaneity, emotion, and freedom of expression that typify many Christian marriages. Should not the closest human relationship on earth inspire us to write poetry, sing songs, and recklessly romance our beloved? See the Song of Solomon! What personalized expression of commitment and appreciation can you share with your spouse today?

4. For some Christians, Genesis 2:23 contains an embarrassing sense of physicality. Bones and flesh are good, but what of mind, heart, and soul? Of course, at one level, we have the literary device of synecdoche here. In synecdoche, the part represents the whole, or the whole the part. So, in commenting on Eve's flesh and bones, Adam affirms the entirety of the woman as his mate. Yet, part of being human is having a body—and one day, we will have resurrection bodies in continuity with our current corporeal existence. For all eternity, we will live in these new, sinless bodies. How then should we treat both our bodies and the bodies of our spouses so that we honor their continuity with eternity?

The Choice to Marry

AMBROSIASTER (C.375)

Ambrosiaster, or Pseudo-Ambrose, is the name given to a collection of commentaries from the early church whose author is unknown. The following passage addresses 1 Corinthians 7:28 and provides a window into how the early church thought of marriage. In the eyes of many, marriage was permitted by God but was considered second-best to a life of celibacy. In the first several centuries of church history, martyrdom was viewed as the ultimate expression of faithfulness to Christ. However, once Christianity became the dominant religion in the Roman Empire, the church began to look to its celibate monks as the exemplars of discipleship.

The man who marries does not sin, because he is doing something which is permitted. But if he refuses to do it, he earns merit and a crown in heaven, for it takes self-control to avoid doing something which is not expressly forbidden.

A virgin who marries is not sinning, because before God this is a matter of free choice. But even though they are free from sin, they will suffer troubles in this world: pains of the womb, the raising of children, making a living, finding somewhere to live, dowries, sickness, household maintenance, the duty of staying closely bound to a wife, the domination of a husband.

Paul is trying to spare them all this when he encourages them to opt for a life which excludes the troubles of the flesh and the above-mentioned anxieties. He is also sparing them in a different way in allowing those who desire what he says is burdensome to have what they want, and not standing in their way.

⤛⤜

Ambrosiaster, *Commentaries on Romans and 1-2 Corinthians*, trans. Gerald L. Bray, Ancient Christian Texts, ed. Thomas C. Oden and Gerald L. Bray (Downers Grove, IL: InterVarsity Press, 2009), 154.

DEVOTION

"God may not give husbands to our daughters," my wife reminded me. "It's possible that they will serve the Lord in singleness all their days." Frankly, the thought (though biblical—and in agreement with Ambrosiaster's quote above) was not something I wanted to hear. I'd rather imagine my daughters happily married to hard-working Christian husbands, with houses full of healthy children.

Paul said in 1 Corinthians 7:7 that he wished all people had the "gift" he had. What is this gift? It is a holy contentedness in his unmarried estate. Paul writes, "Those who marry will have worldly troubles, and I would spare you that" (1 Cor. 7:28). Any pastor, looking across the faces of his congregation, could recount many stories of heart-wrenching suffering, betrayal, and disappointment within the marriages of his flock. The Bible does not sugarcoat the truth—marriage can be immensely joyful (Song 1:1-4), but also can lead to debilitating anxiety and trouble (1 Cor. 7:33-34).

We must be careful not to impose our situations and passions upon the lives of others. While we may not have the gift of singleness, God may give that calling as a life-giving *gift* to a Christian friend, or even to our own children. Ambrosiaster was certainly wrong to value the celibate life too highly, but perhaps contemporary Christians have erred in not valuing it enough.

If, however, you have been given the gift of marriage but are now struggling through the troubles of which Paul warned, remember that God is sovereign and loving. Though you may not now see God's purposes in these marital trials, He is working all things together for your eternal good (Rom. 8:28).

Do not believe the lie that if you had married another person you would not be facing "worldly troubles." In a world of brokenness and sin, a close relationship between two sinners will always have troubles.

Bear With One Another

OPUS IMPERFECTUM (C.400)

Opus Imperfectum is the Latin name given to an incomplete commentary on the book of Matthew that was formerly attributed to John Chrysostom (347-407). Scholars have rejected Chrysostom's authorship since the sixteenth century and now consider the book to be the work of an unidentified fifth-century church leader. Although the commentary is incomplete (addressing only about two-thirds of the Gospel) and bears some marks of aberrant theological influences, it provides helpful insights on particular passages. The quote below, taken from the author's comments on Matthew 5:32, illustrates his desire to prevent couples from pursuing divorce.

But you say, "My wife has many faults." What? You yourself are without fault? If we ought to bear with the imperfections of those outside our family, as the apostle says, "Bear with one another's burdens, and so fulfill the law of Christ," how much more ought we to bear the imperfections of our wives? If someone sees a woman so as to lust after her, he commits adultery with her in his heart; how will he not be condemned for adultery who divorces his wife and gives her the opportunity to commit adultery, so that she commits adultery with another man and the other man with her? For a Christian man ought not only not make himself guilty, but also not give an opportunity for others to make themselves guilty. Otherwise, their offense would overflow into the sin of him who had become the reason for the others to commit their offense.

❧❧❧

"The Twelfth Homily: On Matthew 5," in *Incomplete Commentary on Matthew (Opus Imperfectum)*, trans. James A. Kellerman, ed. Thomas C. Oden, Ancient Christian Texts, ed. Thomas C. Oden and Gerald L. Bray (Downers Grove, IL: InterVarsity Press, 2009), 104.

DEVOTION

"Then Peter came up and said to him, 'Lord, how often will my brother sin against me, and I forgive him? As many as seven times?' Jesus said to him, 'I do not say to you seven times, but seventy-seven times'" (Matt. 18:21-22).

As broken and sin-stained humans, we are creative at justifying our transgressions. We reinterpret God's Word so as to make it less uncomfortable for us. For example, a consistent teaching of Scripture is that we are to bear the inconvenience of others' failings and demands ("bear one another's burdens") so that we might live as Christ's Spirit-led people ("and so fulfill the law of Christ") [Gal. 6:2]. Yet, we somehow think it is OK to grumble and nitpick over the burdens we must bear from our spouses. In the quote above, the author of the *Opus Imperfectum* gives a reminder that for every fault you find in your spouse, he or she could rightly point out a flaw in you!

The gospel of Jesus Christ challenges this kind of sinful "score-keeping." As God has extended His undeserved grace towards us in Christ, so we are to extend it to others (Eph. 4:32). To not offer forgiveness to those who have offended us is to call into question whether we truly know the forgiveness of the Heavenly Father (1 John 3:14-15).

We readily counsel our children about forgiving the classmate who is teasing them. We expect our pastor not to lash out at difficult people at the congregational meeting. We sit in silent disapproval towards the bitter aunt who complains about her daughter. Yet, we ignore our own lack of love, grace, and forgiveness towards the husband or wife God has given us as our most intimate companion. Forgive others seventy-seven times? Of course! But, concerning our husband or wife, we think, "Here we go again ... Do that one more time, and I'll ..."

Where have you failed to show your spouse the basic love and forgiveness that should characterize God's people? What would your marriage look like if you committed to treating your spouse with at least the same level of respect an ordinary Christian should show to a store clerk or mail carrier?

To the experienced husband or wife reading this ... it does not matter if you have decades of dysfunction and neglect behind you. God can begin writing a new story in your marriage today.

MEDIEVAL ERA

(c.500–1400)

Imitate Christ in Loving Your Spouse

GREGORY THE GREAT (540–604)

Born into a wealthy family, Gregory the Great left a promising career in politics to become a monk. After several years of the monastic life, he was elected pope. Although he was at first reluctant to take the position, he eventually transformed the office and cast a long shadow over the papacy throughout the Middle Ages. The following excerpt is taken from his *Book of Pastoral Rule* (c. 590), which was written to guide bishops in their personal conduct and to instruct them in their ministry to others.

For those who are bound in wedlock are to be admonished that, while they take thought for each other's good, they study, both of them, so as to please their companions but not displease their Maker; that they so conduct the things that are of this world as still not to omit desiring the things that are of God; that they so rejoice in present good as still, with earnestness, to fear eternal evil; that they so sorrow for temporal evils as still to fix their hope with entire comfort on everlasting good …

Husbands and wives are to be admonished, that those things wherein they sometimes displease one another they bear with mutual patience, and by mutual exhortations remedy. For it is written, "Bear one another's burdens, and so fulfill the law of Christ" (Gal. 6:2). For the law of Christ is charity; since it has from Him bountifully bestowed on us its good things, and has patiently borne our evil things. We, therefore, then fulfill by imitation the law of Christ, when we both kindly bestow our good things, and piously endure the evil things of our friends. They are also to be admonished to give heed, each of them, not so much to what they have to bear from the other as to what the other has to bear from them. For, if one considers what is borne from one's self, one bears more lightly what one endures from another.

∽≈∽

Gregory the Great, *The Book of Pastoral Rule* 2.26, trans. James Barmby, Nicene & Post-Nicene Fathers (Peabody, MA: Hendrickson, 1889, repr. 2004), 12:56-57.

DEVOTION

Gregory the Great reminds us that a successful, happy marriage is found in embracing your Christian duty to bear with the burdens your spouse causes you. Gregory's instructions are in accord with the words of the Jesus, who commanded, "You shall love your neighbor as yourself" (Matt. 19:19).

A wife might respond, "How can I love my husband when he won't change? Everyday it's the same annoying habits or routine. I wonder if the children will grow up to be losers like him."

A husband might reply, "How can I love her when she is so infuriating? She's an emotional train wreck, constantly sapping my energy and time. Think about the success I could be in work or ministry if it weren't for my wife!"

So, you can't love your spouse because he/she is so undeserving? Well, look to the way you love yourself as a model. In Jesus' command to love one's neighbor (Matt. 19:19), He assumes we love ourselves and then commands us to love others in that same pattern.

Most people really do love themselves. Think about it: when given the chance, you choose "the best" (food, life, salary) for yourself. You hope the best for yourself, and even though you are not what you want to be, you give yourself a second chance ... and then a third chance ... and so on.

What if you extended that same grace to those around you? Perhaps your spouse is so conditioned to your disapproval that it will take some time to convince him/her that you are sincere. Your negative attitude may really be the main problem. Do you stew about the "speck" in your spouse's eye while you have a log sticking out of your own eye (Matt. 7:3-5)?

When the disciples of Jesus love others, the light of the new age shines in the darkness (1 John 2:8). What of your own words and actions today will reveal the light of the coming age shining through your marriage and home?

One Flesh and One Mind

HUGH OF ST. VICTOR (1096–1141)

As the headmaster of an important abbey in Paris, Hugh of St. Victor was one of the most highly respected theologians of the twelfth century. Among his many works, the following quote comes from a letter he wrote to a neighboring bishop. In arguing for the Catholic dogma of Mary's perpetual virginity, Hugh made the point that consent and not consummation make a marriage. Although Protestants would take issue with his larger argument about the mother of Jesus, the following paragraph is a helpful reminder that the biblical concept of being united as "one flesh" speaks to more than a merely physical union.

See now the nature of the contract by which they bind themselves in consented marriage. Henceforth and forever, each shall be to the other as a same self in all sincere love, all careful solicitude, every kindness of affection, in constant compassion, unflagging consolation, and faithful devotedness. And this in such a way that each shall assist the other as being one's own self in every good or evil tiding, the companion and partner of consolation, thus proving that they are united in trial and tribulation. Finally, each one shall attend outwardly to the needs of the other's body, taking it to self as being his own flesh to cherish, and so shall he also attend inwardly to love for the heart, as though it were his own soul to keep in peace and quiet (as far as lies within him) without worry. In this way they shall dwell in the peace of a holy society and the communion of a sweet repose so that it no longer be the one who lives, but the other. Thus each shall live for self even more happily and blessedly. Such are the good things of marriage and the happiness of the chaste society of those who love each other.

∽⧉∾

Hugh of St. Victor, "On the Virginity of the Blessed Virgin Mary," in Jean LeClerq, *Monks on Marriage. A Twelfth-Century View* (New York: The Seabury Press, 1982), 26.

DEVOTION

"It is not good that the man should be alone; I will make him a helper fit for him" (Gen. 2:18).

Humans were not made to live solitary lives. As creatures fashioned in the image of the Triune God (Father, Son, and Spirit), we were created for community. In this broken world, however, we close ourselves off from others. We live shockingly solitary lives even as we are surrounded by other people. Technology further divides us into isolated silos of lonely existence. We hide our fears, struggles, and failures—or we share them with near strangers on the internet. In doing so, we refuse the healing and gracious gift of God that we find in our spiritual brothers and sisters.

If you are married, the closest and deepest spiritual community God has given to you is in your own spouse. As Hugh of St. Victor reminds us above, marriage is not simply the unique sexual relationship shared by husband and wife. Do you and your spouse confess your sins to each other? Do you share your doubts and fears? Do you help each other practically and emotionally in moments of need? Do you pray with and for one another? Do you encourage your spouse when you see signs of God's grace in his/her life?

Perhaps your spouse is sick with a chronic illness or has suffered severe mental or physical decline as the result of aging or an accident. Let the words of Hugh of St. Victor challenge you. Do you "attend outwardly to the needs of the other's body"?

Take a moment to visualize your marriage as a place of deep spiritual friendship and radical self-sacrifice. What specific steps can you take today to move your marriage in that direction?

Neither Queen Nor Slave

PETER LOMBARD (1100–1160)

Peter Lombard was born in Italy but educated in Paris, where he was eventually appointed bishop of the city. Lombard's most significant contribution was his work *The Sentences*, a four-volume theology textbook that organized biblical passages and writings from the church fathers together on particular subjects. Lombard's text was considered the standard systematic theology from the time it was written up to the Reformation. In the section on marriage, from which the following quote is taken, he argued that partnership is at the heart of the relationship.

And because [Eve] is not given as a slave-girl or as one to lord it over him, in the beginning she was not formed either from the highest part, nor from the lowest, but from the side of the man, for the sake of conjugal partnership. If she had been made from the highest, as from the head, she might seem created for domination; but if from the lowest, as from the feet, she might seem to be created for subjection to slavery. But because she is taken as neither your queen, nor your slave-girl, she is made from the middle, that is, from the side, because she is taken for conjugal partnership.

〜〜〜

Peter Lombard, *The Sentences* IV.28.4.1-2, trans. Giulio Silano (Toronto: Pontifical Institute of Mediaeval Studies, 2007), 4:172.
[Language Updated]

DEVOTION

"There is neither Jew nor Greek, there is neither slave nor free, there is no male and female, for you are all one in Christ Jesus" (Gal. 3:28).

Because of the radical feminism in our day, the Christian church can sometimes sound shrill and restrictive when it speaks about marriage or gender. A woman cannot be blamed for remarking, "After reading all these evangelical books on gender, I understand clearly all the things I *cannot* do in the church, but what *can* I do?"

In the Scriptures, God proclaims the equal worth of men and women. Both men and women are created in the image of God. Genesis 1:27 reads: "So God created man in his own image, in the image of God he created him; male and female he created them." Without the woman, the creation is incomplete and "not good" (Gen. 2:18). In the quote above, Peter Lombard is right to assert the equality and value of the woman in such memorable, poetic fashion.

Although God has revealed himself definitively as Father, at times in the Scriptures He uses feminine imagery to describe His care for His people (e.g., Isa. 42:14; 49:14-15). The love, tenderness, and tenacity of a woman are reflections of divine goodness.

In Galatians 3:28 (quoted above), Paul makes clear that men and women stand before God equally as sinners in need of salvation, and equally as brothers and sisters in God's kingdom. A differentiation of roles in the home and church in no way implies a woman's inferiority.

At the same time, let us recognize the many ways the Bible speaks of women acting in the church and home which may challenge our stereotypes. The Proverbs 31 woman is a resourceful and active entrepreneur (Prov. 31:10-31). Paul speaks of women publicly praying or prophesying in the church (1 Cor. 11:5). The deacon Philip had four unmarried daughters who prophesied (Acts 21:9).

Is your own understanding of gender roles shaped more by Scripture or by experience, culture, or family background? Let us celebrate the beautiful image of God that shines through our wives and daughters, affirming their spiritual gifts and equal standing before God in creation and salvation!

Christ's Affirmation of Marriage

GUIBERT OF TOURNAI (c. 1200–1284)

Guibert was a Franciscan monk from Tournai, Belgium, a French village that stands today as one of the two oldest cities in the nation. Guibert was a respected theologian, evidenced by his election to succeed his good friend Bonaventure (1221–1274) as one of the key leaders of the Franciscan movement. In the following excerpt from one of his sermons, Guibert spoke of the significance of Christ's attendance at the wedding at Cana. Even though Guibert himself had renounced the pursuit of marriage for the monastic life, he was eager to affirm the divine approval of those who chose to marry.

Jesus was invited to a marriage, and his disciples too; and when the wine ran out, his mother said to him, "They have no wine" (John 2:2-3). The Lord honoured the partnership of marriage which links man to woman. For this was the first sacrament, and the one instituted and ordained by the Lord from the beginning of the world, and made in the earthly paradise at the beginning of the Old Testament, and confirmed by the Lord in the first miracle which he did in the time of the New Testament. And so he honoured marriage with his bodily presence, with a special miracle, with an unbreakable sacrament: so that just as there is in Christ an inseparability of natures after taking on of flesh, so too in marriage there is a bond of inseparability after the commingling of the flesh. For the Lord knew that there would be certain heretics who would prohibit marriage (1 Tim. 4:3). Therefore, he went in person to a marriage, showing that a woman does not sin if she gets married (1 Cor. 7:28, 36).

❧❧❧

Guibert of Tournai, "Marriage Sermon," in D. L. D'Avray, *Medieval Marriage Sermons. Mass Communication in a Culture without Print* (New York: Oxford University Press, 2001), 301. By permission of Oxford University Press.

DEVOTION

"On the third day there was a wedding at Cana in Galilee, and the mother of Jesus was there.

Jesus also was invited to the wedding with his disciples ... This, the first of his signs, Jesus did at Cana in Galilee, and manifested his glory. And his disciples believed in him" (John 2:1-2, 11).

When you attend an event, you approve of the gathering in some way. A common liturgy for Protestant wedding services, in accord with the words of Guibert of Tournai above, notes that the Lord Jesus blessed the institution of marriage through attending a wedding at Cana.

Jesus' implicit approval of marriage at the Cana wedding is made unmistakably clear from His teaching on the institution in other settings (e.g., Matt. 5:31-32; 19:1-9).

Marriage is God's idea. God made humans as male and female—and God Himself officiated the first marriage, presenting the woman to the man (Gen. 2:22). The Old Testament is replete with regulations for marriage—guarding the sacrosanct emotional and physical dimensions of the relationship (e.g., Lev. 18).

Yet, humans are prone to distort God's good design with labels, limits, and liberties that God has not given. In the quote above, Guibert of Tournai calls marriage a "sacrament"—implying that divine grace is dispensed to the married couple through the operations of an institutional church. Many errors are introduced by this concept of "sacrament." Here we will note two:

1. There is no priestly class that controls the dispensation of grace. In the New Covenant era inaugurated by Jesus, all of God's people are priests (Jer. 31:31-34; 1 Pet. 2:9).

2. Jesus himself is our high priest, who once-for-all gained access for God's people to forgiveness, grace, and righteousness (Heb. 7:27).

Obedience in this life is not a means of making us more acceptable to God in the hereafter. God welcomes us eternally because of Jesus' perfect life and atoning death. That is the gospel (Rom. 3:21-24). Our obedience to God is in response to His gracious love, not the other way around.

Jesus attended the wedding at Cana in Galilee. In some sense, the Lord attended your wedding too (Matt. 28:20). And, if you and your spouse are Christians, the Spirit of God indwells you. Ponder anew your marriage in light of the presence and blessing of the Triune God.

A Good Wife

BARTHOLOMEW OF ENGLAND (c. 1203–1272)

Bartholomew was an English monk who compiled an early forerunner to the modern encyclopedia. *On the Properties of Things* (c. 1260) was one of the most popular books in the medieval world; it was translated and dispersed throughout Europe and provided much of the scientific background for the writings of William Shakespeare (1564–1616). It covered a vast array of subjects including philosophy, medicine, zoology, botany, and, of course, theology. In the excerpt below, Bartholomew reflects on the qualities of a good wife and the great lengths a man is willing to go to in order to secure such a bride for himself.

For in the wedding contract, he gave his word to live with his wife without departing, and to pay her his debt, and to keep her and love her before all others. A man has such great love for his wife that, for her sake, he exposes himself to all dangers; and sets her love before his mother's love; for he dwells with his wife, and leaves his father and mother …

Before the wedding, he does all that he is asked to do for her love and he does it with all his might, denying her nothing she desires. He speaks to her pleasantly, and gazes upon her face with good cheer and a sharp eye. At last, he vows himself to her and announces his promise in the presence of her friends. He confirms his vows with a ring and gives her gifts as a token of his commitment to her. He throws a party to celebrate and afterwards embraces her as his wife.

No man has more wealth, than he that has a good woman for his wife; no man has more woe, than he that has an evil wife … A good wife acts as follows: she is busy and devout in God's service, meek and helpful to her husband, fair and kind to her family, merciful and good to the needy, easy and peaceful to her neighbors, ready, wary, and wise in things that should be avoided, mighty and patient in suffering, busy and diligent in her work, modest in her clothing, sober in her actions, [and] wise with her words … . Such a wife is worthy to be praised, who aims to please her husband with her female duties rather than her braided hairs and with her virtues rather than her fair clothes.

Robert Steele, *Medieval Lore from Bartholomaeus Anglicus* (1893; repr., London: Chatto and Windus, 1907), 56–58.

DEVOTION

In the quote above, Bartholomew speaks of the high level of commitment that one makes in the covenant of marriage. All of the external symbols to which Bartholomew refers (i.e., gifts, rings) represent the couple's abiding promise of a life together in love and sacrificial service.

One of the elements that is often forgotten in the initial declaration of that marital commitment is the commitment one is making to one's in-laws.

Though it is rarely considered prior to marriage, relationships with in-laws can cause a large amount of stress in a marriage. In our individualistic Western society, few people adequately prepare for the way marriage ties them to their spouse's family in a lifelong commitment.

The way forward is not to run away from this struggle, but to seek the Lord's instructions. The Bible commands us to honor our parents, which by extension, includes the parents of our spouse (and the grandparents of our children!). Not only emotional commitment is required, but if necessary, financial support. What if your in-laws have lived irresponsibly and now need basic care? Shouldn't they just reap what they have sown?

The Bible does not require you to send your in-laws to Hawaii, but the Apostle Paul teaches that providing for the basic needs of close relatives is an essential element of faithfulness to Christ. He writes, "But if anyone does not provide for his relatives, and especially for members of his household, he has denied the faith and is worse than an unbeliever" (1 Tim. 5:8).

To covenant in marriage with another person is to commit to care for his or her family. However difficult that obligation might be, where is God calling you to Spirit-empowered obedience?

Commending Marriage

STATUTES OF SALISBURY (c. 1217)

During the Middle Ages, many considered marriage an inferior option for Christians. The unhelpful and unbiblical hierarchy that emerged during the Patristic era persisted, leaving priests in the awkward situation of trying to affirm a life among their parishioners that they had rejected themselves. The following excerpt from a local statute of the English church attempts to guide priests in this endeavor by encouraging them to commend marriage and remind the married in their congregation of the divine purposes for the institution.

Priests ought to take great pains to praise marriage in the highest possible terms and in many ways. Let them stress its inherent worth and the blessings which it brings, and in contrast let them make sexual relations outside of marriage seem vile. Let them boldly claim it as one of the sacraments, which goes back to the very beginning and was first established by the Lord himself in paradise. And since the blessings of marriage are fidelity, offspring, and a mystical symbol—that is, the fidelity of the marriage bed, offspring for the worship of God, and a mystical symbol of Christ and the church—it is clear that marriage is the most desirable, good, and valuable privilege in this life.

❦❦

"First Statutes of Salisbury #82: Concerning the
Commendation of Marriage."
Translation by Tyler Flatt

DEVOTION

"Even before he made the world, God loved us and chose us in Christ to be holy and without fault in his eyes. God decided in advance to adopt us into his own family by bringing us to himself through Jesus Christ. This is what he wanted to do, and it gave him great pleasure" (Eph. 1:4-5 NLT).

A prominent pastor who wrote an influential book on marriage once remarked to me that every marriage in the Bible is dysfunctional. Yet, even with these true-to-life descriptions of marital challenges, the authors of Scripture (like the "Statutes of Salisbury" above!) consistently held marriage in honor as an institution created by God for the good of humanity.

Certainly, we cannot deny many elements of dysfunction in the marriages around us. In light of such ubiquitous failure, it can be tempting to disparage marriage. Marriage is seen either as outdated, or as something that needs to be "expanded" to include all sorts of non-biblical relationships.

The path of faithfulness, however, holds up the beauty of marriage, while also acknowledging that every husband and wife is a flawed sinner that fails to live consistently in obedience to God's instructions.

Every Christian can, however, also say they belong to a flawless family. As noted in the Scripture above (Eph. 1:4-5), we are adopted into God's family. Here we find a perfect heavenly Father who has never sinned against us and will never abandon us.

Did you have an especially difficult family growing up? Are you afraid that you are repeating those same destructive patterns in your new family unit? Don't despair, because you are also part of a new family—the family of God. Your loving heavenly Father will enable you to write a new story that reflects His goodness. And, when you fail, you will teach your family how to repent and live in humility—a lesson that is, in itself, a proclamation of the glorious gospel of Christ.

Should a Man Love His Wife or Parents More?

THOMAS AQUINAS (1225–1275)

Thomas Aquinas was the greatest theologian of the Middle Ages and one of the most influential Christian thinkers of all time. The Dominican friar possessed a brilliant mind, which he used to engage the writings of non-Christians such as the ancient Greek philosopher Aristotle. In his massive tome *Summa Theologica*, which he did not finish before his death, Thomas addressed a host of issues, including the question below about who deserved a man's supreme earthly love: his wife or his parents. Thomas' answer illustrates the way he sought to apply both reason and revelation to the questions of Christianity.

It would seem that a man should love his wife more than he loves his father and mother, since no one parts with anything unless it is because he loves something else more. But in Genesis 2:24 it says that a man will leave his father and mother on account of his wife; therefore he should love his wife more than he loves his father or mother.

Moreover, the Apostle says in Ephesians 5:33 that "husbands should love their wives as themselves." But a man should love himself more than he loves his parents; therefore he should also love his wife more than he loves his parents.

Moreover, love should be greater where there are more reasons for love. And in the friendship between husband and wife there are more reasons for love, since as Aristotle says in his Ethics this kind of friendship is characterized by utility, pleasure, and virtue, if the spouses are virtuous. Therefore a man's love for his wife should be greater than his love for his parents...

In sum, we should say that the appropriate degree of love can be considered both in terms of the motive of the Good as well as in relational terms. Thus, in terms of the Good—which is the ultimate goal of love— parents should be loved more than wives, since our love for parents is motivated by a certain original and more lofty Good. Yet in relational terms the wife should be loved more, since a wife is united to her husband as one flesh, according to Matthew 19:6, "So they are no longer two but one flesh." Hence the wife should be loved more ardently, but greater reverence should be shown to parents.

Thomas Aquinas, "Treatise on Faith, Hope and Charity, Question 26, Article 11," in *Summa Theologica*. Translation by Tyler Flatt.

DEVOTION

"Therefore shall a man leave his father and his mother, and shall cleave unto his wife: and they shall be one flesh" (Gen. 2:24 KJV).

Thomas Aquinas reminds us that the Bible's call for a husband or wife to "leave" parents and "cleave" to their spouse is an action expressing ultimate loyalty and love. Instructions to leave and cleave are often repeated in Christian marriage books, but what does this "leaving" and "cleaving" practically look like?

It's important to recognize the inescapable cultural elements in "leaving." In some cultures and times, the newly married couple lives with the son's parents until they die. Many traditional cultures based around agriculture or animal husbandry continue to follow this tight-knit extended family structure.

Yet, even if husband and wife live in the same building as their parents, they must still "leave" that prior parent-child relationship. The newly married couple's ultimate loyalty and concern are no longer to their parents, but to each other. That does not mean indifference towards their parents. Far from it! Children are called to honor their parents all their lives. Yet, when it comes to decisions about where to live, employment, medical treatment, children, or parenting, only two people are allowed into the "inner sanctum" of decision making—husband and wife.

Secondly, what does it look like to "cleave"? Of course, most literally, a husband and wife cleave to one another physically in their intimate expression of married love. Such physical intimacy is to be found exclusively and joyfully only within the holy covenant of marriage. Alongside that physical cleaving, however, husband and wife are to exhibit a broader relational cleaving. Is the wife weighed down over a trying relationship? Her husband must also carry this burden. Is a husband troubled by an injustice he suffered at work? With his wife's loving support, a man can bear it.

Some married couples (metaphorically-speaking) keep one foot in their parents' home. This failure to "leave and cleave" will make the other spouse feel unsettled. It is possible for couples who have been married for decades to still have "leave and cleave" problems.

Have you embraced the Bible's instructions to "leave and cleave"? If not, where is God calling you to step into radical commitment and oneness with your spouse?

Become the Kind of Person You Want to Marry

BERNADINO OF SIENA (1380–1444)

Bernadino of Siena was known as "the Apostle of Italy" for his frequent and extensive missionary travels across the nation. The Franciscan monk began his ministry in his native Siena when he began to lead a local hospital charged with caring for the city's plague-stricken citizens. From there, he traveled the country preaching moral reform. In the following excerpt, Bernadino chastises those who desire more from their spouse than they are willing to be themselves, a problem as common today as it apparently was in the fifteenth century.

Do you wish your wife to be faithful to you? Then you keep faith with her. There are many who will not take wives, and cannot find them. Do you know why? Because a man will say: I want a wise woman, while all the time he himself is a fool. That is not right. Fool must wed with fool. And you, what kind of a wife do you want? … How do you want your wife to be? You want her honest. And you yourself are dishonest. Again, what kind of a wife do you want? A temperate one. And you yourself are never seen outside the tavern. You will not find one to your taste. And you, what wife do you want? An industrious one. And yet you waste the whole day. What do you want? A peaceable wife. And you are a man who would pick a quarrel with a straw if it pricked your foot in the road. And what wife do you want? An obedient one. And yet you have never obeyed your mother or your father or any other person. You don't deserve one. Finally, what wife do you want? Oh, one that is good and beautiful and wise, in fact one that has all the virtues. Well, I tell you that if you want such a one so you must be yourself, for if you expect her to be virtuous, good, and beautiful, be sure she will expect the same of you.

～≫≪～

Bernadino of Siena, "Choosing a Wife," in *Examples of San Bernardino*, trans. Ada Harrison (London: Howe, 1926), 117-18.

DEVOTION

"An excellent wife who can find? She is far more precious than jewels" (Prov. 31:10).

"Her husband is known in the gates when he sits among the elders of the land" (Prov. 31:23).

For a young man or woman seeking a godly, responsible spouse, Bernadino of Siena's advice is excellent: seek to be the kind of spouse whom another mature Christian would want to marry. It is no surprise in Proverbs 31 (quoted above) that the excellent wife ("far more precious than jewels") is married to an influential, leading man ("who sits among the elders of the land").

At the same time, sometimes one spouse will mature tremendously after marriage while another spouse flounders in irresponsibility or spiritual malaise. Do you get up early and accomplish a day's work before your spouse rolls out of bed to watch TV? Is your Bible well-worn, while your spouse hunts for their Bible once a week on Sunday morning?

In such a situation, first, you should ask God to reveal any judgmentalism in your own life. A difference in temperaments, sleep patterns, or devotional reading is not necessarily a sign of sin. Are you, perhaps, walking around with a log in your eye trying to remove a speck from your brother's eye (Matt. 7:3)?

Second, you should pray for your spouse. Ask the Lord specifically and repeatedly to reveal to them their sin—so that they can repent and grow in spiritual health and fruitfulness (Luke 18:1; 1 John 5:16).

Third, by the example of your life, you should demonstrate what an excellent spouse looks like (1 Pet. 3:1-6). If your husband or wife is not a believer, perhaps you will have the joy of seeing them come to Christ. If they are a believer, then expect to see God working to grow and mature them. Remember, any fruit in your own life is not an opportunity to be proud or compare yourself with others, but to give glory to God for the work He is doing in you by His Spirit (1 Cor. 4:7).

REFORMATION &
PURITAN ERA

(c. 1400–1700)

How to Improve Your Husband

DESIDERIUS ERASMUS (1466–1536)

The Dutch humanist Desiderius Erasmus was known for his clever writing and scholastic aptitude. His most significant contribution to the church was his edition of the Greek New Testament (first edition, 1516), which he hoped would be translated into every language of the world. Erasmus was appreciated for both his wisdom and his wit. The following conversation is excerpted from a fictional dialogue between two troubled women discussing how to navigate a difficult marriage. According to Eulalia, a woman ought to weigh a man's faults before she marries him, but once married, it is "time for improving him, not blaming him."

Xanthippe: Do you get along well with your husband?

Eulalia: Everything's peaceful now.

Xanthippe: There was some turmoil at first, then?

Eulalia: Never a storm, but slight clouds appeared occasionally; the usual human experience. They could have caused a storm had they not been met with forbearance. Each of us has his own ways and opinions, and—to tell the truth—his own peculiar faults. If there's any place where one has a duty to recognize these, not resent them, surely it's in marriage.

Xanthippe: Good advice.

Eulalia: It frequently happens, however, that good will between husband and wife breaks down before they know each other well enough. This above all is to be avoided, for once contention arises love is not easily recovered, especially if the affair reaches the point of harsh abuse. Things glued together are easily separated if you shake them immediately, but once the glue has dried they stick together as firmly as anything. Hence at the very outset no pains should be spared to establish and cement good will between husband and wife. This is accomplished mainly by submissiveness and courtesy, for good will won merely by beauty of person is usually short-lived.

Xanthippe: But tell me, please, by what arts you draw your husband to your ways.

Eulalia: I'll tell you in order that you may imitate them … My first concern was to be agreeable to my husband in every respect, so as not to cause him any annoyance. I noted his mood and feeling; I noted the circumstances too, and what soothed and irritated him … When he's at leisure and not disturbed, worried, or tipsy … admonish him politely, or rather entreat him—in private—to take better care of his property, reputation, or health in one respect or another. And this very admonition should be seasoned with wit and pleasantries … After reproving him as I intended, I'd break off that talk and turn to other, more cheerful topics. For as a rule, my dear Xanthippe, our mistake is that once we've started to talk we can't stop.

Xanthippe: So they say.

Eulalia: Above all I was careful not to scold my husband in the presence of others or to carry any complaint farther than the front door. Trouble's sooner mended if it's limited to two.

Erasmus, "The Wife Blaming Her Marriage," in *The Colloquies* (1518). Taken from *The Book of Marriage. The Wisest Answers to the Toughest Questions*, ed. Dana Mack and David Blankenhorn (Grand Rapids: William B. Eerdmans Publishing, 2001), 102.

DEVOTION

"Older women likewise are to be reverent in behavior, not slanderers or slaves to much wine. They are to teach what is good, and so train the young women to love their husbands and children, to be self-controlled, pure, working at home, kind, and submissive to their own husbands, that the word of God may not be reviled" (Titus 2:3–5).

Many women might roll their eyes when they discover that the fictitious dialogue between Xanthippe and Eulalia above was written by a priest in the sixteenth century.

With divine wisdom, however, in Titus 2:3-5, Paul commands older women (not men!) to instruct younger women in the practical matters of married life. Older women can speak with both a scriptural and an experiential authority. They can say, "I know being a wife and mother is hard (because I am one), but God is calling you to submit to your husband and love your children. And, by God's grace, you can do this."

Are you a younger woman? Find an older woman who can speak into your life. When you arrive on her doorstep, come not only with questions, but with real friendship that gives as well as receives. (For example, bring fresh-baked bread, her favorite coffee, or offer to help her in some practical way.)

Perhaps you have successfully navigated life experiences that are leaving younger women exasperated (e.g., new marriage, in-laws, young children, teenagers). Is the Lord calling you to mentor a younger woman in the practical matters of life? Did a specific person come to your mind? Reach out to her today. The Lord has designed the church to pass down wisdom from one generation to the next in this way.

What the World says about Marriage

MARTIN LUTHER (1483–1546)

When Martin Luther nailed his ninety-five theses to the door of the church at Wittenberg in 1517, the German monk famously declared his theological disagreements with the Roman Catholic Church. Although his marriage to a runaway nun some eight years later is less talked about today, it was nearly as revolutionary at the time. When Luther married Katharina von Bora (1499–1552), he demonstrated the far-reaching social implications of the Protestant Reformation and gave the Christian world something it hadn't seen in centuries: a significant leader who was also a husband and father.

In order that we may not proceed as blindly, but rather conduct ourselves in a Christian manner, hold fast first of all to this, that man and woman are the work of God. Keep a tight rein on your heart and lips; do not criticize his work, or call that evil which he himself has called good. He knows better than you yourself what is good and to your benefit, as he says in Genesis [2:18], "It is not good that the man should be alone; I will make him a helper fit for him." There you see that he calls the woman good, a helper. If you deem it otherwise, it is certainly your own fault, you neither understand nor believe God's word and work. See, with this statement of God one stops the mouths of all those who criticize and censure marriage.

For this reason young men should be on their guard when they read pagan books and hear the common complaints about marriage, lest they inhale poison. For the estate of marriage does not set well with the devil, because it is God's good will and work. This is why the devil has contrived to have so much shouted and written in the world against the institution of marriage, to frighten men away from this godly life and entangle them in a web of fornication and secret sins. Indeed, it seems to me that even Solomon ... was speaking against just such blasphemers when he said in Proverbs 18:22, "He who finds a wife finds a good thing, and obtains favor from the Lord." What is this good thing and this favor? Let us see.

The world says of marriage, "Brief is the joy, lasting the bitterness." Let them say what they please; what God wills and creates is bound to be a laughingstock to them ... The estate of marriage is something quite different from merely being married ... Now the ones who recognize the estate of marriage are those who firmly believe that God himself instituted it, brought husband and wife together, and ordained that they should beget children and care for them. For this they have God's word, and they can be certain that he does not lie. They can therefore also be certain that the estate of marriage and everything that goes with it in the way of conduct, works, and suffering is pleasing to God.

Martin Luther, "The Estate of Marriage, 1522," trans. and ed. Walther I. Brandt, *Luther's Works*, ed. Helmut T. Lehmann (Philadelphia: Muhlenberg Press, 1962), 45:37-38.

DEVOTION

"He who finds a wife finds a good thing and obtains favor from the LORD" (Prov. 18:22).

Throughout the day, what script runs through your head about your spouse? Do you think things like, "Not again!" Do you mutter insults under your breath after hanging up the phone with your husband or wife? Do you think or say, "I can't believe my wife/husband is so [*fill in the blank*]?"

If you view your spouse as an annoyance, you will end up treating him/her as an irritation, and your marriage will be filled with strife, disappointment, and sadness.

Luther realistically described marriage as filled with sacrifice and suffering, yet marriage is God's mysterious plan for providing the world with a daily mini-drama of the relationship between Christ and the church (Eph. 5:21-33).

This week, be conscious of the script that runs through your head about your spouse. If you are not thinking or saying true and godly things, ask God to forgive you. Look to Christ, who makes both you and your spouse acceptable on the basis of His perfect life and sacrificial death. Memorize one of the following Scriptures and say it to yourself when your mind begins to fall into the rut of criticism: Genesis 2:18 or Proverbs 18:22.

A Reformation Definition of Marriage

HEINRICH BULLINGER (1504–1575)

Heinrich Bullinger was one of the most influential voices of the second generation of Protestant Reformers, especially in Switzerland where he took over the pulpit of the great Ulrich Zwingli (1484–1531). In his four decades of pastoral ministry, Bullinger was known for his powerful preaching and for his compassion toward the downtrodden, which included some of the Puritans fleeing persecution in England. Bullinger married a former nun named Anna and the two had eleven children together, including six sons who became Protestant pastors. In the quote below, Bullinger defines marriage and its purposes, illustrating the perspective of the Reformers.

Wedlock, which is also called matrimony, is an alliance or holy joining together of man and woman, coupled and brought into one by mutual consent of them both, to the intent that they, using all things in common between themselves, may live in chastity, and train up their children in the fear of the Lord ... God, according to his natural goodness, directs all his ordinances to the great good and abundant commodity of mortal men. Therefore it follows, that he ordained matrimony for the preservation of mankind, to the end that man's life might be pleasant, sweet, and thoroughly furnished with joys sufficient. But all these causes may be reduced into the number of three.

First, God himself doth say, "It is not good for man to be alone; let us make him an helper therefore to be before him," or to dwell with him. So, then, the first cause why wedlock was instituted is man's pleasure, that thereby the life of man might be the more pleasant and more enjoyable ... The second cause why matrimony was ordained is the begetting of children for the preservation of mankind by increase, and the bringing of them up in the fear of the Lord: for the Lord blessed Adam and Eve, saying, "Increase and multiply, and replenish the earth" ... . The third cause why matrimony was ordained the Apostle Paul expressed in these words: "To avoid whoredom, let every man have his own wife, and every woman her own husband" ... . By this we learn, that the sexual relations of a man with his own wife are not reputed for a fault or uncleanness in the sight of God. Whoredom is uncleanness in the eyes of the Lord, because it is directly contrary to the law of God: but God hath allowed wedlock and blessed it; therefore married folks are sanctified by the blessing of God through faith and obedience.

〜〜〜

Heinrich Bullinger, *The Decades of Henry Bullinger*, trans. H. I., ed. Thomas Harding (Cambridge: University Press, 1849), 1:394, 397, 400-401. [Language Updated]

DEVOTION

"For it is better to marry than to burn with passion" (1 Cor. 7:9).

I (Rob) was surprised to find this quote adorning the front of a wedding program.

"Isn't that a bit too explicit?" I thought.

The apostle Paul did not think so, as is clear from his instructions to the Corinthians. Indeed, in this portion of his letter, Paul gives many explicit instructions about sex. Paul writes the following:

- Because of the broken world in which we live, both men and women can expect to face regular temptation to sexual sin (1 Cor. 7:2). Both single and married persons should anticipate deceptive allurements to non-marital (and thus forbidden) sexual experiences—lust, pornography, pre-marital sex, etc.

- One of the purposes of marriage is that the husband and wife can meet the sexual needs and desires of the other within the God-ordained sphere of marriage (1 Cor. 7:2).

- Only in the taking of a "personal prayer retreat," and with the mutual consent of both the husband and wife, should there be even a temporary pause in regular marital sex (1 Cor. 7:5).

- To neglect regular sex in marriage is to open the door to the devil's destruction of your marriage through sexual temptation (1 Cor. 7:5).

Five centuries ago, Heinrich Bullinger, in Pauline fashion, noted that one of the purposes of marriage is to help husbands and wives "avoid whoredom." Can we be any less explicit or deliberate? Are you following Paul's instructions about sex in your marriage?

Peace Leads to Prayer

JOHN CALVIN (1509–1564)

Best known for the theological movement associated with his name, John Calvin served as a pastor and spiritual leader in Geneva, Switzerland, for almost three decades. Calvin's *Institutes of the Christian Religion* (first edition, 1536), which he continued to work on for over twenty years, set forth a distinctly Protestant approach to theology and profoundly influenced subsequent generations. His biblical commentaries are still appreciated today for their rich exegetical insights and pastoral wisdom. In the following explanation of 1 Peter 3:7, Calvin displayed his practicality in warning couples about how their relationship with one another could impact their relationship with God.

For God cannot be rightly called upon, unless our minds be calm and peaceable. Among strife and contentions there is no place for prayer. Peter indeed addresses the husband and the wife, when he bids them to be at peace one with another, so that they might with one mind pray to God. But we may hence gather a general doctrine—that no one ought to come to God except he is united to his brethren. Then as this reason ought to restrain all domestic quarrels and strifes, in order that each one of the family may pray to God; so in common life it ought to be as it were a bridle to check all contentions. For we are more than insane, if we knowingly and willfully close up the way to God's presence by prayer, since this is the only asylum of our salvation.

John Calvin, *Commentaries on the Catholic Epistles*, Calvin's Commentaries, trans. and ed. John Owen (Edinburgh: Calvin Translation Society, 1855; repr., Baker Books, 1999), 22:100.

DEVOTION

"Likewise, husbands, live with your wives in an understanding way, showing honor to the woman as the weaker vessel, since they are heirs with you of the grace of life, so that your prayers may not be hindered" (1 Pet. 3:7).

John Stott once observed, "Obedience is the indispensable condition, not the meritorious cause, of answered prayer."

Husband, if you are a Christian, you have no choice but to love your wife and treat her with kindness. Otherwise, you are putting yourself under God's fatherly discipline. And, your soul will find no rest until, by the power of the Holy Spirit, you repent of your harshness and seek to "live with your wife in an understanding way" (1 Pet. 3:7). John Calvin is right; since God tells us that harshness with our wives closes the way to God in prayer, only a fool would willfully choose this path!

Wife, if you are a Christian, you have no choice but to respect and submit to your husband. Do you wonder why God feels distant and is not responding to your prayers? Is the Lord drawing your attention to your rebellious attitude?

To all spouses, know that God wants you to reconcile with your closest Christian brother or sister (that is, your spouse) before you approach His altar (Matt. 5:24). Meditate on Jesus' Parable of the Unforgiving Servant:

> Then his master summoned him and said to him, 'You wicked servant! I forgave you all that debt because you pleaded with me. And should not you have had mercy on your fellow servant, as I had mercy on you?' And in anger his master delivered him to the jailers, until he should pay all his debt. So also my heavenly Father will do to every one of you, if you do not forgive your brother from your heart (Matt. 18:32-35).

Dearly Beloved

THE BOOK OF COMMON PRAYER (1559)

The Book of Common Prayer is a liturgical guide for the Church of England that contains instructions for daily, weekly, and annual services of worship as well as specific ceremonies such as weddings. It was originally compiled in the sixteenth century by Archbishop Thomas Cranmer (1489-1556) to provide a simple, biblical liturgy in the English language. After various edits in the centuries that followed, the book remains in use today and continues to impact the structure and language of weddings around the world, even those outside of the Anglican tradition. The following paragraph opens the official wedding service and provides an overview of marriage from a sixteenth-century perspective.

Dearly beloved friends, we are gathered together here in the sight of God, and in the face of his congregation, to join together this man and this woman in holy matrimony, which is an honorable estate, instituted by God in paradise during man's innocency, signifying to us the mystical union between Christ and his church, which Christ adorned and beautified with his presence and first miracle he performed at the wedding in Cana of Galilee, and is commended by Saint Paul to be honorable among all men. As such, it is not to be entered into carelessly, lightly, or wantonly, to satisfy man's carnal lusts and appetites, like brute beasts that have no understanding, but reverently, discreetly, wisely, soberly, and in the fear of God, duly considering the causes for which matrimony was ordained. Its first purpose was the procreation of children to be brought up in the fear and nurture of the Lord and to the praise of God. Second, it was ordained for a remedy against sin, and to avoid fornication, that such persons who do not have the gift of continency might marry, and keep themselves undefiled members of Christ's body. Thirdly, it was created for the mutual society, help, and comfort, that the one ought to have of the other, both in prosperity and adversity. Into this holy estate, these two persons have now come to be joined. Therefore, if any man can show any just cause why they should not be lawfully joined together, let him now speak, or forever hold his peace.

⌦⌦⌦

The Book of Common Prayer 1559, ed. John E. Booty (Washington, DC: Folger Shakespeare Library, 1976), 290–91. [Language Updated]

DEVOTION

When you think back to your wedding day, can you see the many friends and family in attendance? Don't forget the invisible presence of the most honored guest at your wedding—God Himself.

In the traditional wording of the marriage ceremony from *The Book of Common Prayer*, the wedding couple is reminded that they are not only in the presence of God's people, but more importantly, are "gathered together here in the sight of God."

If the President of the United States or the Queen of England had attended your wedding, think how honored you would have felt! Now, imagine that great person moved into your home, daily asked you about your marriage, and offered to help you in your relationship. The comparison breaks down (you may not care for the President's marriage advice), but the analogy reminds us of the personal presence of God both at our wedding ceremony and in our daily married life.

Remember these truths: God created the institution of marriage, your sacred promise of faithfulness was made in His presence, and it is He Himself who dwells within you and enables the fulfillment of that covenant.

The Bible also teaches us that God is a holy God who holds accountable all who break their marriage covenant. "Let marriage be held in honor among all, and let the marriage bed be undefiled, for God will judge the sexually immoral and adulterous" (Heb. 13:4).

In the quotation from the Book of Common Prayer above, what phrase or description is most striking to you?

As you think on these things, may the Holy Spirit stir you toward the faithfulness you vowed to your spouse on your wedding day.

A Good Wife is a Gift from God

THOMAS GATAKER (1574–1654)

Thomas Gataker was an English Puritan who served on the Westminster Assembly. The Puritans were instrumental in helping the church develop a biblical perspective on marriage in the sixteenth and seventeenth centuries. For centuries, theologians had taught that the production of children was the primary purpose of marriage. The Puritans, on the other hand, emphasized that affection between the spouses served as its own independent good. As Gataker's quote below illustrates, they were eager to give God the glory for the many blessings of marriage.

Is a good wife such a special gift of God? Then marriage is unquestionably a blessing, and no small one, in itself, but one of the greatest outward blessings that man enjoys in this world …

The wife comes first, as the first and principal blessing, and the children come next … . If children are a blessing, then the root from whence they spring ought to be much more esteemed … . Children are the gift of God; but the wife is a more special gift of God; she comes in the first place, they in the second …

Again, is a good wife such a special gift of God? Then if we find in marriage inconveniences, hindrances, distractions, and disturbances, let us learn to what we must ascribe them. Not to God's gift or ordinance but to man's corruption—abusing God's gift, perverting God's ordinance, and turning to his own evil what God has given him for his good. For there is nothing that comes from God but that which is good. But as pure water may be tainted by the pipe that conveys it, and the sun beams receive a tint from the colored glass that they pass through, so our foul hands and filthy fingers often soil and sully God's ordinances. Our filth and corruption often taint and infect them, so that they lose not only much of their natural grace, and are so strangely transformed that God himself can scarcely discern his own [image] in them, but also they lose their fruit and efficacy, becoming evil instead of good.

Thomas Gataker, *A Good Wife God's Gift* (London: John Haviland, 1623), 11-14. [Language Updated]

DEVOTION

"Houses and wealth are inherited from parents, but a prudent wife is from the LORD" (Prov. 19:14 NIV).

In Proverbs 19:14, the ancient biblical author notes that parents pass along wealth to their children (sons in Ancient Near Eastern culture) after their death. This is generally true. Parents sacrifice and save, bequeathing material resources to their children. There are exceptions, however. A parent may die owing money and pass along only headaches to their heirs.

In the Ancient Near East, if a son was without wealthy parents, it was virtually impossible that he would ever be rich. Whether a man's family was rich or poor, however, his parents could never guarantee the blessing of a wise wife. The Lord, who alone sees the hearts of humans, and holds all things under His sovereign power, should be looked to as the provider of a prudent wife. Several points of application come to mind:

1. If you are not married, look to the Lord as the provider of your future spouse. Pray fervently for a godly spouse. Don't despair about your geographical location or current relationships. The provider of wise spouses is not bound by such limitations.

2. If you are married to a wise spouse, thank the Lord. As Thomas Gataker notes, your spouse is "one of the greatest outward blessings that [a person] enjoys in this world." You do not deserve the spouse you have. Just as inherited riches are the fruit of another's labor, your spouse's holiness is the work of God's Spirit in his/her life. Your marriage and spouse are a gift from God.

3. If you do not think that your spouse deserves the adjective "prudent" (Prov. 19:14), remember that the Lord is in the business of taking the lowly and foolish things of the world and transforming them into the image of His Son (1 Cor. 1:26-28).

4. Marriage is a great leveler among an otherwise stratified society. A wise spouse can be a source of great joy and temporal peace to even the most impoverished or downtrodden. A wicked spouse, on the other hand, can make bitter the blessings of wealth and comfort. "It is better to live in a corner of the housetop than in a house shared with a quarrelsome wife" (Prov. 21:9).

In moments of complete honesty, would your spouse call you "prudent" (Prov. 19:14) or "quarrelsome" (Prov. 21:9)? After answering this question, ask yourself a second: How sure are you that you perceive your own behavior rightly? Ask for God's grace to see yourself as He sees you and to follow the leading of His Spirit in repentance and obedience.

Season your Actions with Love

WILLIAM GOUGE (1575–1653)

William Gouge was an influential Puritan who served the congregation of St. Anne Blackfriars in London for over forty-five years, published a number of significant doctrinal works, and helped draft the *Westminster Confession of Faith* (1646). His best-known publication is an extensive study of family life entitled, *Of Domesticall Duties* (1622), from which the following quote is taken. As a father of thirteen and a devoted husband, Gouge combined faithful exegesis with the wisdom he had developed through years of applying biblical principles in his own home.

No duty on the husband's part can be rightly performed except it be seasoned with love ... His look, his speech, his carriage, and all his actions, wherein he hath to do with his wife, must be seasoned with love; love must show itself in his commandments, in his reproofs, in his instructions, in his admonitions, in his authority, in his familiarity, when they are alone together, when they are in company, before others, in civil affairs, in religious matters, at all times, in all things. As salt must be first and last upon the table, and eaten with every bit of meat, so must love be first in an husband's heart, and last out of it, and mixed with everything he hath to do with his wife.

∽≈≈≈∾

William Gouge, *Of Domesticall Duties* (London: John Haviland, 1622), 351-52.

DEVOTION

"And Leah conceived and bore a son, and she called his name Reuben, for she said, 'Because the LORD has looked upon my affliction; for now my husband will love me'" (Gen. 29:32).

William Gouge's description of marital love is touching, but it may be difficult to read for someone married to an unloving spouse. Consider the biblical example of Leah. In Genesis 29:32 we peer into the relational dysfunction of the patriarchs. Leah was, of course, one of Jacob's two wives. She was the "unloved" of the two and is repeatedly described as longing for her husband's affections. In this verse, she thinks that by birthing a male heir (important in an Ancient Near Eastern context), she would earn the affection of her husband.

The biblical narrative never indicates that Leah received the affection she craved. Even in his old age, Jacob continued to favor the children of his other wife, Rachel (who by then had died in childbirth of her second son, Benjamin).

Even in the midst of repeated human sin and family dysfunction, the Lord was fulfilling His gracious promises to Abraham's descendants. Amazingly, after being sold into slavery by his brothers, Joseph could later look back at the wicked things they had done and say to them, "As for you, you meant evil against me, but God meant it for good" (Gen. 50:20).

What relational or family dysfunction are you experiencing right now? Be encouraged that God works through such circumstances for our good and His glory. Is there some way that your spouse is mistreating you, through words or deeds? By faith, one day, you too can say to those who are now hurting you, "You meant evil against me, but God meant it for good."

Guarding Against the Enemy

JOHN MILTON (1608–1674)

The Puritan poet John Milton penned one of the finest epic poems in the history of the English language. *Paradise Lost* (1667), which Milton dictated in his final years after his vision had failed, is a reimagining of the early chapters of Genesis focusing on the consequences of man's disobedience. In the excerpt below, Adam warned Eve of the dangers of straying alone in the Garden due to the presence of the "malicious Foe" who sought to destroy their peaceful existence. Milton was all too familiar with Satan's efforts to "disturb Conjugal Love" having suffered through an unhappy marriage himself.

[Adam speaking to Eve, attempting to convince her to stay with him in the Garden lest the Enemy draw her away into sin]

But if much converse perhaps
Thee satiate, to short absence I could yield.
For Solitude sometimes is best society,
And short retirement urges sweet return.
But other doubt possesses me, lest harm
Befall thee sever'd from me; for thou know'st
What hath been warn'd us, what malicious Foe
Envying our happiness, and of his own
Despairing, seeks to work us woe and shame
By sly assault; and somewhere nigh at hand
Watches, no doubt, with greedy hope to find
His wish and best advantage, us asunder,
Hopeless to circumvent us join'd, where each
To other speedy aid might lend at need;
Whether his first design be to withdraw
Our fealty from God, or to disturb
Conjugal Love, than which perhaps no bliss
Enjoy'd by us excites his envy more;
Or this, or worse, leave not the faithful side
That gave thee being, still shades thee and protects.
The Wife, where danger or dishonour lurks,
Safest and seemliest by her Husband stays,
Who guards her, or with her the worst endures.

John Milton, *Paradise Lost*, Book IX, lines 247-69, ed. James Boyd (New York: A.S. Barnes & Co., 1870), 376-77.

DEVOTION

"For the husband is the head of the wife even as Christ is the head of the church, his body, and is himself its Savior" (Eph. 5:23).

The Bible teaches a man is to be head of the home, but what that actually means is more elusive. Distortions abound. Being head of the home does not mean the husband gets to sit in a recliner and watch TV while his wife brings him cold drinks!

In Ephesians 5:23, Paul compares the husband's headship to the headship of Christ. We discover that marital headship means the following: (1) The wife is to submit lovingly to the husband's authority. (2) The husband must love his wife sacrificially in the pattern of Jesus' love for the church. (3) The husband should consider his wife's needs as though they were the needs of his own body. (4) The husband is to care for and cherish his wife. (5) The husband is to guard the unique one-flesh relationship with his wife. (6) The husband is to act towards his wife so that their marriage proclaims the truth about the way Christ loves the church.

The Bible does not record many things that happened in the Garden of Eden. It does not record Adam's conveying of God's instructions to Eve about the forbidden fruit, nor any other warnings he might have given her. In fact, we know very little about what the headship of the first husband looked like. However, with sanctified imagination, John Milton creatively portrayed the love and protection of Adam as head of Eve prior to their fall into sin.

In this broken world, men too often domineer (abusing their headship) or retreat in passivity (abdicating their headship). God calls men to Spirit-empowered, Christ-like, sacrificial headship. Husbands, are you protecting your families? Wives, are you following your husband's leadership?

To My Dear and Loving Husband

ANNE BRADSTREET (1612–1672)

Anne Bradstreet was the first woman in the American colonies to publish a book of poetry. A devout Puritan and mother of eight, her collection includes a number of works addressed to her family. The following verses were penned in honor of her husband Simon Bradstreet (1604-1697), who served as governor of the Massachusetts Bay Colony. This short poem offers a glimpse into Puritan thinking on the goodness and goals of marriage, as well as a portrait of one bride's joy in her groom.

If ever two were one, then surely we.
If ever man were loved by wife, then thee;
If ever wife was happy in a man,
Compare with me ye women if you can.
I prize thy love more than whole mines of gold,
Or all the riches that the East doth hold.
My love is such that rivers cannot quench,
Nor ought but love from thee give recompense.
Thy love is such I can no way repay;
The heavens reward thee manifold, I pray.
Then while we live, in love let's so persevere,
That when we live no more we may live ever.

Anne Bradstreet, *The Works of Anne Bradstreet in Prose and Verse*, ed. John Harvard Ellis (Charlestown, MA: Abram E. Cutter, 1867), 394.

DEVOTION

Have you ever seen a husband neglect his wife's needs to the point where he crushes or embitters her? Paul commands husbands to consider the emotional, physical, and spiritual needs of their wives (Eph. 5:28-29). A wife's needs should be so incorporated into her husband's consciousness that they become his needs. "Husbands should love their wives as their own bodies. He who loves his wife loves himself" (Eph. 5:28).

Have you ever seen a wife repeatedly correct or criticize her husband—to the point where you cringe at her words? Paul tells wives to submit to and respect their husbands (Eph. 5:22, 33). A woman, through her words and actions, will either build up her home or tear it to the ground (Prov. 14:1).

In the poem above, Anne Bradstreet pictures the loving respect a wife should give to her husband—even if he does not deserve it, which he frequently will not! Compare Bradstreet's poem to the bitter comments spouses mutter under their breaths about each other.

Wife, ask a family friend how you can show more loving respect to your husband through your words and actions. Husband, ask a family friend how you can better care for your wife's needs. Or, perhaps, married couple, ask each other. Listen, learn, and by the power of God's Spirit, repent and be transformed.

A Puritan's Advice for Getting Along With Your Spouse

RICHARD BAXTER (1615–1691)

For almost twenty years, Richard Baxter pastored a Nonconformist congregation in Kidderminster, England. Although his country was in civil war and he endured frequent religious persecutions, his ministry was instrumental in transforming the town. In his late forties he married a woman converted under his preaching named Margaret Charlton (1639-1681), who proved to be a faithful wife and helpful partner in ministry. Baxter's classic work *A Christian Directory* (1654) addresses a host of practical topics related to piety, including the following tips to help Christian couples get along.

1. Keep up your conjugal love in a constant heat and vigour.
2. Both husband and wife must mortify their pride and passion, which are the causes of impatience; and must pray and labour for a humble, meek, and quiet spirit.
3. Remember still that you are both diseased persons, full of infirmities; and therefore expect the fruit of those infirmities in each other; and make not a strange matter of it, as if you had never known of it before.
4. Remember still that you are one flesh; and therefore be no more offended with the words or failings of each other, than you would be if they were your own.
5. Agree together beforehand, that when one is in the diseased, angry fit, the other shall silently and gently bear, till it be past and you are come to yourselves again.
6. Look before you, and remember that you must live together until death, and must be the companions of each other's fortunes, and the comforts of each other's lives, and then you will see how absurd it is for you to disagree and vex each other.
7. As far as you are able, avoid all occasions of wrath and falling out, about the matters of your families.
8. If you cannot quickly quench your passion, yet at least refrain your tongues; speak not reproachful or provoking words. Talking it out hotly blows the fire, and increases the flame; be but silent, and you will sooner return to your serenity and peace.
9. Let the sober party condescend to speak fairly and to entreat the other (unless it be with a person so insolent as will be the worse).
10. Confess your fault to one another, when passion has prevailed against you; and ask forgiveness of each other, and join in prayer to God for pardon.

Richard Baxter, *A Christian Directory* in *The Practical Works of Richard Baxter* (London: George Virtue, 1838; repr., Soli Deo Gloria Publications, 2008), 433-34.

DEVOTION

The Bible is full of practical instruction about how to live together in unity, love and wisdom with other humans—despite being sinners living in a broken world. Richard Baxter's advice provides a nice synthesis of several practical biblical teachings on relationships.

One motif in his advice deals with speech. Indeed, husbands and wives could, with great benefit, meditate on the many biblical proverbs about speech.

One such proverb is: "Where words are many, sin is not absent, but he who holds his tongue is wise" (Prov. 10:19 NIV). Husband or wife, how many times has the fragile glass of marital unity been shattered because you have not restrained your speech?

As Christians, we must recognize that though we belong to God and are forgiven of our sin, our minds are not totally purified in this life. We are called to actively "put to death the misdeeds of the body" (Rom. 8:13). The Christian life is, as Luther put it, one of "continual repentance," living in Christ's forgiveness as we acknowledge our sins.

Perhaps one of the healthiest things you could do for your marriage is to ask for God's grace to speak less. Though your heart continues to think of hurtful things (and the devil may whisper such thoughts in your ear as well), you are called to resist the temptation to say those things. "Let no corrupting talk come out of your mouths, but only such as is good for building up, as fits the occasion, that it may give grace to those who hear" (Eph. 4:29). Pray for God's ability to perceive your words as He hears them.

When contentious or harmful thoughts come to mind, silently pray, "God, please forgive me for wanting to hurt my spouse with my words or to stir up strife. By the power of your Spirit, help me to hold my tongue. Give me words of healing and grace that have the aroma of the gospel of Christ."

Saying a Final Farewell

SARAH GOODHUE (1641–1681)

From what we know of her, Sarah Goodhue was a typical Puritan wife in colonial America. Her daily life consisted of caring for her family—which eventually included ten children—alongside her husband, Joseph, who was a deacon in the town church of Ipswich, Massachusetts. The following quotation is taken from a letter Sarah wrote to her husband and children when she began to sense a "strong persuasion" of her impending death. As she affirmed her love for her family, she also dispensed advice for their future without her. Her letter was later published when her premonition proved accurate and she died suddenly, a mere three days after giving birth to twins.

A tender-hearted, affectionate and entirely loving husband you have been to me in many ways. If I could but speak of what I have found as to these outward things; I being but weak in nature. In all my burdens you have willingly sympathized with me, and cheerfully you have helped me bear them; even though I was but weak natured and so the more unable to go through those troubles in my way. Yet you have by your cheerful love to me helped me forward in a cheerful frame of spirit and have taken great pains and care for the good of my soul.

These twenty years of experiencing your love to me in this way has so ingrained it upon my mind, that I do think that there never was a man more truly kind to a woman. I desire forever to bless and praise the Lord, that in mercy to my soul, He by His providence ordered that I should live with you in such a relation. Therefore, dear husband, be comforted in this: if God providentially breaks the relationship between us that He created, know that you have been a man of knowledge to me, faithfully discharging to God and my soul your Scripture-commanded duty. Now you may behold with comfort the effects which the grace of God has wrought in me. Our prayers have not been hindered but a gracious answer has come from the Lord, which is of great price and reward. Although my departure be your loss, yet I trust in and through Jesus Christ, it will be my gain.

❧❧

The Copy of a Valedictory and Monitory Writing Left by Sarah Goodhue
(Cambridge: n.p., 1681), 12. [Language Updated]

DEVOTION

"For to me to live is Christ, and to die is gain. If I am to live in the flesh, that means fruitful labor for me. Yet which I shall choose I cannot tell. I am hard pressed between the two. My desire is to depart and be with Christ, for that is far better" (Phil. 1:21-23).

Paul had an overflowing, genuine, passionate love for the congregations to which he wrote. He also valued something more than them. He knew that being with Christ and dwelling with the Lord for eternity made all other relationships pale in comparison. Sarah Goodhue, in her letter above, affirms this same truth, noting that her impending death would truly be her "gain."

When one of my daughters was very young she had trouble getting her mind around this truth. "I love God more than you!" she would say provocatively, looking to me for both approval and explanation. At one level, she understood that she was called to love God more than anyone or anything else, but by her oddly-timed declaration, she indicated this assertion was something that did not quite fit her reality.

There are probably some people reading this devotional who think it's acceptable to love your family more than God. After all, didn't God create family? And like the bumper sticker says, "Family is forever!"

Actually, family is not forever. The Psalmist writes, "For my father and my mother have forsaken me, but the LORD will take me in" (Ps. 27:10). In Isaiah 49:15 the Lord declares, "Can a woman forget her nursing child, that she should have no compassion on the son of her womb? Even these may forget, yet I will not forget you."

Loving our spouse or children more than God is actually harmful to them. We become idolaters—looking to other humans for ultimate meaning and significance—a smothering, unbearable burden to finite creatures.

When we love God as the highest and chief love, we place Him at the center of the "solar system" of our affections in such a way that all other relationships are free to orbit as intended. And on that day when we face our death, we, like Sarah Goodhue, can bless our families with words that not only show our great love for them, but also our ultimate love for our Lord and Savior.

The Householder's Psalm

MATTHEW HENRY (1662–1714)

Matthew Henry was a Puritan pastor well-known for his sound exegesis and practical preaching. His *Exposition of the Old and New Testaments* is one of the most popular commentaries of all time and continues to be used by pastors even today. Henry, who pastored a congregation in Chester, England, for much of his ministry, was also a devoted family man. According to his biographers, he prayed with his family each morning, reviewed sermons with them throughout the week, and catechized his children in the evenings. The following quote, taken from his commentary on Psalm 101, illustrates his commitment to being a spiritual leader in his home.

David here [in Psalm 101] cuts out to himself and others a pattern of both a good magistrate and a good master of a family; and, if these were careful to discharge the duty of their place, it would contribute very much to a universal reformation.

Observe … the general resolution David took up to conduct himself carefully and conscientiously in his court (v. 2) … not only how he would walk when he appeared in public, when he sat in the throne, but how he would *walk within his house*, where he was more out of the eye of the world, but where he still saw himself under the eye of God. It is not enough to put on our religion when we go abroad and appear before men; but we must govern ourselves by it in our families. Those that are in public stations are not thereby excused from care in governing their families; nay, rather, they are more concerned to set a good example of *ruling their own houses well* (1 Tim. 3:4). David had his hands full of public affairs, yet he returned to bless his house (2 Sam. 6:20). He resolves: To act conscientiously and with integrity, to *walk in a perfect way*, in the way of God's commandments; that is *a perfect way*, for *the law of the Lord is perfect*. In this he will walk *with a perfect heart*, with all sincerity, not dissembling either with God or men. When we make the word of God our rule, and are ruled by it, the glory of God our end, and aim at it, then we walk *in a perfect way with a perfect heart*.

❧❧❧

Matthew Henry, *Commentary on the Whole Bible* (1706; repr., Peabody, MA: Hendrickson, 1991), 887.

DEVOTION

"He must manage his own household well, with all dignity keeping his children submissive, for if someone does not know how to manage his own household, how will he care for God's church?" (1 Tim. 3:4-5)

Matthew Henry is right to call on men to lead their families spiritually. Indeed, it is not uncommon in modern evangelical churches for men to be exhorted to lead their families. Yet, what does this mean? Below are some practical expressions that family leadership can take:

Make sure your family attends a Bible-believing church and spends time around God's people. In committing to a church, have you chosen social relationships over spiritual truth? Or, have you perhaps "neglected meeting together" with God's people (Heb. 10:25)—instead spending your weekends at the lake or at sporting events? What priorities are your children unconsciously absorbing from you? Where there are behavioral or spiritual needs in your family, address them. Do not passively surrender your wife or children to whatever influences happen to be blowing through their lives. If you feel incompetent to help your wife or children, ask a mature Christian brother. Read good Christian books on parenting and marriage. Read a chapter of the book of Proverbs daily. What does it say about life, money, marriage, diligence, children, and business? By the power of God's Spirit, seek to be a man who is characterized by a wise life—and who overflows with that wisdom to his wife and children. Resolve with King David and the Puritan Matthew Henry to "walk with integrity of heart within [your] house."

EARLY
EVANGELICAL
ERA
(c. 1700–1900)

I Hope You Will Lead Me to God

PHILIP DODDRIDGE (1702–1751)

The eighteenth-century pastor Philip Doddridge was a man of many skills. In addition to being a pastor and a hymn writer, he was also an educator and author. His most famous work, *The Rise and Progress of Religion in the Soul* (1745), was treasured in its day and influential in the piety of many, as was his multi-volume guide for family worship (*Family Expositor*, 1739). He also seems to have had an exemplary marriage. Doddridge and his wife, Mercy (1709-1790), sought to encourage one another in their relationship with God even before they were married, as the following excerpt from their correspondence illustrates.

Had I the most ample time, all I could say would be utterly insufficient to express the sense I entertain of your worth, and the warmth of my gratitude for the obliging reception you gave me. Words cannot express it; but my heart feels it so tenderly, that it often throbs with joy and fondness. Will you be mine? I think it is presumption to hope it. I fear I shall over-love you; and then perhaps God will afflict you. That is the only way in which I can fear being afflicted in you; as we must be in everything which we suffer to usurp the place of God in our hearts. But I hope you will rather lead me to Him. I am sure it ought to be so; for I am fully conscious that it was He, that gave you that lovely form, that intelligence, that wisdom, generosity, and goodness, without which your beauty and your wit might have tormented, but would never have made me happy. It was He, that opened to me a heart which the greatest and best of men could hardly have deserved; and kindly disposed events, by His Providence, in a manner favourable to my dearest wishes. And is He to be forgotten and neglected in, and for this? No, my dearest, it shall not be.

When I possess you, I am sure you will endeavour to raise my soul to Him; and I will endeavour to improve my hopes of you to the same happy purpose … When I consider the glories of the heavenly world, I hardly dare to imagine they are designed for me. But I am unworthy of so much excellence as He bestows in you; and can the more easily believe, that He will give me heaven at last, when He is now giving me so much, in the enjoyment of one, who seems already fit to be its inhabitant. I write my heart; call it not flattery.

❦

Philip Doddridge, "Letter to Mercy Maris, October 23, 1730," in *The Correspondence and Diary of Philip Doddridge, D. D. Illustrative of Various Particulars in his Life hitherto Unknown: with Many Notices of his Contemporaries; and a Sketch of the Ecclesiastical History of the Times in which he Lived*, ed. John Doddridge Humphreys (London: Henry Colburn and Richard Bentley, 1830), 3:46.

DEVOTION

Nothing other than a Spirit-empowered commitment to the will of God will guarantee the longevity and health of a marriage.

At the same time, no husband wants to hear his wife say, "I hate living with you, but I will never leave you because I obey God."

Though all marriages go through challenges and disappointments, God created marriage to be a place of mutual pleasure and comfort. Philip Doddridge's quote reminds us of the playful and tender words that should be found between a husband and wife.

When the first woman was brought to the first man, he broke out in exultant verse, "This at last is bone of my bones and flesh of my flesh; she shall be called Woman, because she was taken out of Man" (Gen. 2:23).

Scholars debate the meaning of the Song of Solomon. Does the book give us a metaphorical description of Christ's love for the church? Is it about God's love for ancient Israel? A straightforward reading of the book, however, discovers passionate and romantic poetry between a husband and his wife.

At one point, the young husband says to his bride, "How beautiful and pleasant you are, O loved one, with all your delights! Your stature is like a palm tree, and your breasts are like its clusters. I say I will climb the palm tree and lay hold of its fruit. Oh may your breasts be like clusters of the vine, and the scent of your breath like apples, and your mouth like the best wine. It goes down smoothly for my beloved, gliding over lips and teeth" (Song. 7:6-9).

The Song of Solomon reminds us that it was God's idea to create sexual passion and romantic love. Within marriage, sexual pleasure and romance are beautiful and blessed by God.

Husband and wife, ask for God's grace to enjoy the mutual delights and pleasures of marriage! Read the Song of Solomon together. Compose some of your own romantic poetry! Speak words to your spouse that are so expressive and joy-filled that you will have to say, like Philip Doddridge, "I write my heart; call it not flattery."

Give My Kindest Love to My Dear Wife

JONATHAN EDWARDS (1703–1758)

Jonathan Edwards was possibly the most brilliant mind America ever produced. While he is best known for his classic sermon, "Sinners in the Hands of an Angry God," his many other works such as *Religious Affections* (1754) and *Freedom of the Will* (1754) were significant during the Great Awakening and beyond. In addition to his legacy as a pastor and theologian, Edwards also set a solid example in his family. There is no stronger evidence for his devotion to his family than the following two excerpts, which contain his final words regarding his wife and her response to his unexpected death.

[Jonathan Edwards' words to his daughter, Lucy, on his deathbed:]

Dear Lucy, It seems to me to be the will of God, that I must shortly leave you; therefore give my kindest love to my dear wife, and tell her, that the uncommon union, which has so long subsisted between us, has been of such a nature, as I trust is spiritual, and therefore will continue forever; and I hope she will be supported under so great a trial, and submit cheerfully to the will of God. And as to my children, you are now like to be left fatherless; which I hope will be an inducement to you all, to seek a Father who will never fail you.

[Sarah Edwards to her daughter, Esther:]

O my very Dear Child,
What shall I say? A holy and good God has covered us with a dark cloud. O that we may all kiss the rod and lay our hands on our mouths. The Lord has done it. He has made me adore his goodness that we had him so long. But my God lives and he has my heart. O what a legacy my husband and your father has left us. We are all given to God and there I am and love to be.

❧❧

Taken from George M. Marsden, *Jonathan Edwards: A Life* (New Haven, CT: Yale University Press, 2003), 494-95.

DEVOTION

It is unlikely that you and your spouse will die at the same moment. Just as in the case of Sarah and Jonathan Edwards, one of you will likely precede the other. Let's imagine for a moment, that you are the first to pass into eternity. If God gives you the chance to say goodbye in that last moment of life on this earth, what would you say? What regrets would you have? What would you wish you could have said or done earlier?

In a recent article, pastor R. C. Sproul, Jr. said that his greatest regret after his wife's death was not holding her hand more often. Life is so fast-paced and demanding that urgent matters crowd out important things. You must be vigilant and proactive to spend this short life in light of the eternity that stretches out before you. Ten billion years from now, imagine you could look back and talk to yourself on this very day. How would you advise yourself to speak and act towards your family?

In Psalm 90:12 Moses prays, "Teach us to number our days that we may get a heart of wisdom."

Let Moses' words be your prayer today. What if your wife were taken from you in a horrid accident tomorrow? What tenderness do you wish you could have shown her today? What words of healing, forgiveness, or appreciation would you wish you could have expressed? Don't hesitate. Live in light of eternity now. *Carpe diem!* (Seize the day!)

A Visit with the Edwards Family

GEORGE WHITEFIELD (1714–1770)

George Whitefield was a British evangelist whom God used as a key instrument in the eighteenth-century revival known as the Great Awakening. Whitefield traveled throughout the English-speaking world, preaching over 18,000 sermons and seeing thousands converted through his ministry. By his own admission, one of his most memorable experiences was a visit he made to the church and home of Jonathan Edwards (1703-1758), an influential pastor in Northampton, Massachusetts. As Whitefield recorded in his journal, the sight of Edwards' family life left an indelible impact on him and the character of Sarah Edwards (1710-1758) in particular made him long for a wife of his own.

Mr Edwards is a solid, excellent Christian, but, at present weak in body. I think I have not seen his fellow in all New England ... At Mr Edwards' request, I spoke to his little children, who were much affected ... I felt great satisfaction in being at the house of Mr Edwards. A sweeter couple I have not yet seen. Their children were not dressed in silks and satins, but plain, as become the children of those who, in all things, ought to be examples of Christian simplicity. Mrs Edwards is adorned with a meek and quiet spirit; she talked solidly of the things of God, and seemed to be such a helpmeet for her husband, that she caused me to renew those prayers, which, for some months, I have put up to God, that he would be pleased to send me a daughter of Abraham to be my wife. Lord, I desire to have no choice of my own. You know my circumstances; You know I only desire to marry in and for You. You did choose a Rebecca for Isaac; choose one to be a helpmeet for me, in carrying on that great work which is committed to my charge.

George Whitefield's Journal (London: Banner of Truth Trust, 1960), 476-77.

DEVOTION

"Elders should be without fault. They should be faithful to their spouse, and have faithful children who can't be accused of self-indulgence or rebelliousness" (Titus 1:6 CEB).

Except for the ability to teach (1 Tim. 3:2), all qualifications given for elders in the New Testament are character qualities that should be true, in growing capacities, of all Christians. Indeed, no Christian should get drunk or be greedy (Titus 1:7). Likewise, here in Titus 1:6, though the instructions are explicitly tied to elders, all Christian men are called to demonstrate faithfulness to their wives and effective leadership/discipline of their children. George Whitefield's description of Jonathan Edwards's family gives us a testimony of a home life so ordered.

The modern world compartmentalizes life. We celebrate someone as a great actor or businessman, while ignoring the wrecked marriages and traumatized children discarded in the wake of worldly success.

Biblically, a "blameless" man is first defined by loyalty to his wife (Titus 1:6). Second, an elder's true character and ability to lead/teach God's people is revealed by his impact on the children in his own home (1 Tim. 3:4-5).

All of us will struggle with failure and disappointment in our roles as spouses and parents. But, looking over our entire lives, would someone say we have been faithful to our spouses? Though we may struggle terribly, have we taken up the mantle to lead, teach, and discipline our children?

Consider your faithfulness to your spouse and your guidance of your children. Where do you need to repent? Where do you need fresh empowering and vision from God's Spirit? "Ask and it will be given to you, seek and you shall find, knock and the door will be opened to you" (Matt. 7:7).

A Firmer Basis

HENRY VENN (1725–1797)

Henry Venn was an influential Anglican bishop during the Evangelical Awakening. Venn was involved in founding the Clapham Sect, a group of mission-minded evangelicals whose most famous member, William Wilberforce (1759-1833), helped end the British slave trade. Venn's most significant work, *The Complete Duty of Man* (1763), was a popular guidebook to the Christian life that explored various topics. In the excerpt below, Venn makes a profound point regarding the only one true foundation on which healthy marriages can rest.

The affection of Christian husbands and wives must be established upon a firmer basis. The husband must love his wife, not only for the charms of her person, the sweetness of her manners, or even the affection he knows she bears him but, above all, because their supreme Benefactor, the Lord of heaven and earth, has said, "Husband, love your wives." The Christian wife must also love her husband principally in obedience to the divine will; not on account of the superiority of his understanding, the applause he receives, the honor of his condition, or the cordiality of his affections towards herself. For if conjugal love be not secured by conscience towards God, a thousand various incidents may make that union miserable which was happy before. Some sudden storm of contention may arise, violent enough to tear up natural affection by the roots. Some bitter expressions may escape in the heat of passion, which shall eat in secret as a canker, and destroy all confidence and peace.

Husbands and wives, on the contrary, in whose hearts the love and authority of God reign, will be united together by the common object of their highest adoration and all-sufficient happiness; they will find their affection, like the law of their God, which has bound them in so close an alliance, constant and unalterable.

❧❧❧

Henry Venn, *The Complete Duty of Man* (London: n.p., 1763), 272.

DEVOTION

"And this is the confidence that we have toward him, that if we ask anything according to his will he hears us. And if we know that he hears us in whatever we ask, we know that we have the requests that we have asked of him. If anyone sees his brother committing a sin not leading to death, he shall ask, and God will give him life" (1 John 5:14-16a).

As Henry Venn notes above, Christian husbands are commanded to love their wives and Christian wives are commanded to respect their husbands (Eph. 5:25, 33).

Yet, every husband and wife will face situations where their spouse fails to keep God's command to love/respect them. What should they do in this situation? Sometimes there will be a need to confront. Sometimes there will be a need to seek outside counsel. There will always be a need to pray. As Venn makes clear, such moments require spouses to base their commitments on a firmer foundation than their own fleeting emotions.

As 1 John 5:14-16 explains, part of God's will for Christians involves helping one another away from destructive sin. When you see another Christian sinning, you should pray for them. It is God's will for that Christian to repent of their sins and be restored to life-giving fellowship with the heavenly Father.

Have you experienced such deep emotional wounds from your husband or wife that you are no longer thinking of him or her as your Christian brother or sister? Ask for God's grace to see your spouse as your spiritual sibling. Rather than focusing on the emotional wound you have received, be concerned with their spiritual condition. Pray fervently and expect the Holy Spirit to bring conviction, repentance, and life. If you have given up all hope of your spouse changing, what does your hopelessness say about your lack of faith in God's transforming power? If these words do not relate to your own marriage, perhaps you could pray for a couple today who may need God to work in their hearts in this way.

The Family as a Preview of Heaven

SAMUEL STENNETT (1727–1795)

Samuel Stennett was a fourth-generation Baptist minister and popular hymn writer in eighteenth-century England. Some of his hymns, such as "Majestic Sweetness Sits Enthroned" and "On Jordan's Stormy Banks," are still sung today. In addition to pastoring the Baptist church at Little Wild Street in London for nearly forty years, he published several influential works, including a family handbook entitled, *Discourses on Domestic Duties* (1783). In the following passage, Stennett sketches a portrait of an ideal family and reflects on the way that a godly home previews heaven.

The father was a wise, affectionate, good man; a sincere disciple of the meek and lowly Jesus, whose doctrine he professed, and whose example he followed ... The welfare of those entrusted to his care, lay near his heart, and ... The counsels of divine wisdom ... were sweetly mingled with the most pleasing expressions of paternal tenderness and love ... The partner of his life, inexpressibly dear to him, had all the charms which virtue and religion could add to a form that commanded admiration and love. She was modest, prudent, and kind ... Nor was she less attentive than he to the duties she owed to God ... Their children (for they had a numerous family) inherited the virtues of their parents, as well as a striking resemblance of their persons...and as the powers of reason expanded, the seeds of religion, which had been carefully sown in their breasts, sprung up under a divine influence, and promised a fair and joyful harvest. They knew, they felt, they acknowledged their ignorance, guilt, and depravity, and looked for pardon and eternal life through the mediation and grace of the Lord Jesus Christ ... And so they were happy, in a degree, beyond what is usual in the present life ... They grew in wisdom and virtue; and conversing daily with heaven in the duties of religion, they were gradually prepared for the sublime services and joys of that better world ... A family, a pious family [such as this], is a shadow, of which heaven is the substance. Visit the pleasant mansion wherein the God of grace chooses to dwell, and say whether you are not struck at your very entrance with this prophetic inscription written in fair characters upon it: "This is the gate of heaven."

❦

Samuel Stennett, *Discourses on Domestic Duties* (1783; repr., Edinburgh: n.p., 1800), 447-50, 469.

DEVOTION

Sometimes active Christians and "full-time" ministers fail to enlist their spouses and children in the ministry alongside them. Rather than living life together under the reign of Christ, ministry becomes something that takes one member of the family away and breeds resentment among the family members who are left. Samuel Stennett, on the other hand, describes a Christian family in which "the children [inherit] the virtues of their parents."

Undoubtedly, ministry requires a sacrifice that sometimes affects those closest to us. Paul notes that husbands and wives, with mutual consent, can choose to refrain for limited times from sexual intimacy so as to devote that time to prayer (1 Cor. 7:5). Jesus speaks of the relational sacrifice required to be His faithful disciples in this world (Luke 14:26).

Yet, the Bible is also full of incidental evidence that early Christians enlisted their families in their ministries.

Paul commented that married apostles traveled with their wives (1 Cor. 9:5). In various gatherings in Acts, entire families are described as gathered together—where they all hear the word of God, believe, and are baptized (e.g., Acts 10:24, 44; 16:15, 33-34; 18:8). In Acts 21:5, Luke personally recollects, "When our days there were ended, we departed and went on our journey, and they all, with wives and children, accompanied us until we were outside the city. And kneeling down on the beach, we prayed."

When Paul writes to the early church leader Philemon, he also mentions Apphia and Archippus as laboring alongside Philemon (Philem. vv. 1-2). Many scholars think that Apphia was Philemon's wife and Archippus was his son.

If you are reading this devotional, you are likely a "serious Christian." Perhaps you have some position of leadership or service in your church. As much as you are able, have you pursued that church ministry so as to involve your spouse and children? Do they view ministry in competition to your commitment to them? Or is your ministry pulling your family into the flowing stream of God's grace?

Have you ever talked to a man or woman who grew up in a home where caring for the poor or hosting traveling missionaries was as common as watching Sunday football games for many families today? What spiritual legacy are you creating with your spouse to pass along to the next generation?

Concern for Newlyweds

ESTHER EDWARDS BURR (1732–1758)

Esther Edwards Burr was the daughter of the most significant theologian in American history, Jonathan Edwards (1703–1758), as well as the mother of future U. S. Vice-President Aaron Burr, Jr. (1756–1836). For at least three years of her life, she kept a detailed journal, which she exchanged with her best friend, Sarah Prince (1728–1771), on a regular basis. The journal provides a rare glimpse into the life of an eighteenth-century American woman as well as a fascinating perspective on the world around her. In the excerpt below, Esther expresses her pity for newly-wedded couples and muses about the challenges they will undoubtedly face.

Been this P. M. to make a wedding visit to a young newly married pair—the woman got a good husband, and I hope he a good wife, but that I am not certain of—I can't help feeling a tender concern for new married people, first because their happiness much depends on their conduct towards each other when first married. Now they begin to discover that they are not perfect, and until now most are apt to think that the party beloved has no faults. It requires some degree of prudence in a woman that has been always served with the greatest kindness and as if she was an absolute Monarch, to be gently blamed in some pretty artful way now that he is her Head and Governor. On the other hand, the husband has need of his share of good temper, when the wife that has always been seen in makeup grows careless of her looks and seems more concerned to appear decent before anybody else other than her husband. Each observes the alteration. The wife supposes his affections cooling, the husband concludes she has more respect for others than him, and when it has gone thus far, you may guess where it is likely to end.

Secondly (sermon wise), I pity them because most have no notion of the new trials that encumber this new state, even though such trials are perhaps not as great as what they endured when they were single. Yet, since they do not expect them, and do not have experience with them, they do not know how to conduct themselves, and instead grow peevish, and injure themselves with the chain that ought to be a silken cord of mutual love and tender sympathy and affection.

Thirdly, the greater part of the world has no sense of the duties of this state, or indeed that there is any duty in the case toward each other, but alas, how are the poor things mistaken. All relative duties are great, but of the nearest and dearest relation must certainly be very great indeed. God must help for we can't fulfill any part of it!

❦❦❦

"June 21, 1757," in *The Journal of Esther Edwards Burr 1754-1757*, eds. Carol F. Karlsen and Laurie Crumpacker (New Haven/London: Yale University Press, 1984), 265–66. [Language Updated]

DEVOTION

"Whoever walks with the wise becomes wise, but the companion of fools will suffer harm" (Prov. 13:20).

Turn on the TV, read an article on the Internet, or talk to a co-worker and you will find plenty of ideas that will drive you away from your spouse.

- "You are not being treated as well as you deserve."

- "There are plenty of other handsome (or beautiful) men/women out there who are more worthy of spending their life with you."

- "When the marriage is not working out, why keep trying?"

- "You married the wrong person, or for the wrong reasons. Divorce him/her and move on."

These are all lies. But if you surround yourself with people who repeat such ideas (even licensed counselors!), the falsehoods will eventually sound right. And in our mobile, affluent, post-Christian society, it has never been easier to find a new community that will affirm whatever lifestyle you choose.

The correspondence between Esther Edwards Burr and Sarah Prince reminds us of the importance of being part of a genuine Christian community. Only there will you will hear the Word of God preached and taught. You will be encouraged to treasure that Word in your heart. You will have people around you who will speak the truth in love to you.

How desperately we need fellow Christian travelers in this life—people whom we can imitate (1 Cor. 11:1), and those who will rescue us like a burning stick from the fire if necessary (Jude 23).

There are also plenty of Christian voices from the past we can learn from. In each generation, God has raised up faithful preachers, teachers, and prophetic truth-tellers (Eph. 4:11-13). We are surrounded by a great cloud of faithful witnesses who successfully finished the race (Heb. 12:1). Esther Edwards Burr is one of those voices. Will we allow her wise observations to shape our understanding of marriage, or will we reflect the "spirit of the age"?

Why God Created the Woman

ANDREW FULLER (1754–1815)

Andrew Fuller was an eighteenth-century British Baptist pastor. At a time when many in his denomination allowed doctrinal error to justify evangelistic apathy, Fuller helped ignite the modern mission movement through his influential work, *The Gospel Worthy of All Acceptation* (1785), and through his leadership in the Baptist Missionary Society that commissioned William Carey (1761-1834) to India. A commentary on Genesis drawn from his sermons provides the following quote, in which Fuller reflects on the creation of the first woman and how a godly relationship between husband and wife distinguishes Christianity from other religions.

The subject closes with a more particular account of the creation of woman. We had a general one before (Gen. 1:27) but now we are led to see the reasons of it. Observe: it was not only for the propagation of the human race, but a most distinguished provision for human happiness. The woman was made for the man; not merely for the gratification of his appetites, but of his rational and social nature. It was not good that man should be alone; and therefore a helper that should be meet, or suitable was given him.

The place assigned to the woman in pagan and Muslim countries has been highly degrading; and the place assigned her by modern unbelievers is not much better. Christianity is the only religion that conforms to the original design that confines men to one wife and that teaches them to treat her with propriety. Go among the enemies of the gospel, and you shall see the woman either reduced to abject slavery, or basely flattered for the vilest of purposes; but in Christian families you may see her treated with honour and respect; treated as a friend, as naturally an equal, a soother of man's cares, a softener of his griefs, and a partner of his joys.

❧❧❧

Andrew Fuller, *Discourses on Genesis* in *The Complete Works of Andrew Fuller* (Philadelphia: American Baptist Publication Society, 1845; repr., Harrisonburg, VA: Sprinkle, 1988), 3:9-10.

DEVOTION

"Then the LORD God said, 'It is not good that the man should be alone; I will make him a helper fit for him'" (Gen. 2:18).

Atheists explain marriage as an accommodation of biological impulses to societal constraints. God tells us that marriage is (among other things) His good gift of companionship to humanity. As Andrew Fuller notes, when a society properly values women as created in the image of God and of equal worth with men, the human race flourishes.

Genesis 2:18 is the first place where the biblical author tells us that something is "not good" in God's creation. Man, as the crown of God's creation, stands incomplete. Without the woman by his side as helper and co-ruler over creation, the man is alone. The man's physical, relational, emotional, and spiritual self is incomplete without a lifelong complementary companion. God does not leave the man in this state of incompleteness; God says He Himself will make a companion who will perfectly meet the man's needs. And, the man in turn will meet her needs. Single reader, do not despair; through God's personal presence in your life and the spiritual family He gives you in the church, He has provided you the wholeness you need as well.

Other family relationships and friendships are a gift from God, but there is a unique and sacred way in which God has ordained your spouse to fit you. If you force a jigsaw puzzle piece into the wrong place, you damage many pieces. Similarly, if you neglect your spouse (the God-given place for physical and romantic companionship) and seek such fulfillment in other relationships, you and others will be damaged.

Have you *relationally* served your spouse (and been served by your spouse) in the way God intends? Are there other relationships in your life that are a threat to your marriage bond? What specific steps will you take to celebrate and to guard the sacred companionship God has given you in marriage?

Can You Part With Your Daughter?

ADONIRAM JUDSON (1788–1850)

Adoniram Judson was America's best-known missionary from the nineteenth century. He served among the Burmese people (in modern-day Myanmar) for nearly forty years. Despite numerous personal tragedies, illnesses, and imprisonments, Judson persevered in Burma and left a legacy that continues to this day. The following excerpt comes from a letter to Judson's future father-in-law, in which he sought the hand of Ann Hasseltine (1789–1826) in marriage, despite the dangers that lay before them both. Adoniram and Ann did eventually marry and subsequently set sail for Burma on February 19, 1812, a mere two weeks after their wedding.

I have now to ask whether you can consent to part with your daughter early next spring, to see her no more in this world? Whether you can consent to her departure to a heathen land, and her subjection to the hardships and sufferings of a missionary life? Whether you can consent to her exposure to the dangers of the ocean; to the fatal influence of the southern climate of India; to every kind of want and distress; to degradation, insult, persecution, and perhaps a violent death?

Can you consent to all this, for the sake of Him who left His heavenly home and died for her and for you; for the sake of perishing, immortal souls; for the sake of Zion and the glory of God? Can you consent to all this, in hope of soon meeting your daughter in the world of glory, with a crown of righteousness brightened by the acclamations of praise which shall resound to her Saviour from heathens saved, through her means, from eternal woe and despair?

〰〰

Edward Judson, *Adoniram Judson, D. D. His Life and Labours*
(London: Hodder and Stoughton, 1883), 20.

DEVOTION

"And they lived happily ever after." Fairy tales and Hollywood movies lead us to believe that marriage is a life of continual bliss. The Bible is more realistic. When two sinners come together in marriage, they will regularly sin against one another, and because of their unique needs and weaknesses, they will also frequently inconvenience each other. In 1 Corinthians 7, Paul encourages those gifted with singleness to embrace the single life for undistracted service to the Lord. Few people are so constituted (1 Cor. 7:6-7). Most will marry, and Paul warns, "Those who marry will have worldly troubles" (1 Cor. 7:28).

People who enter marriage with unrealistic expectations often live in disillusionment and regret. Married persons must embrace this truth: all marriages have challenges and sorrows. But if such challenges are met with faith in God and a commitment to one's spouse, a beautiful picture of Christ's unwavering love for the church becomes visible (Eph. 5:22-33).

In the letter above from Adoniram Judson to his future father-in-law, Judson considers more than the ordinary trials of marriage. As a missionary to difficult lands in the 1800s, Judson knew his upcoming married life would entail suffering and perhaps even death. He wanted to make sure his future bride (and bride's family) had a realistic picture of that life.

Whether your current suffering is a malaria infection while laboring alongside your missionary spouse in Africa, the fatigue of caring for a special needs child in Alabama, or a much more ordinary challenge, ask for God's grace to approach the trials of married life with both realism and faith.

On Marrying a Minister

CHARLES HADDON SPURGEON (1834–1892)

Charles Haddon Spurgeon was the pastor of what became the Metropolitan Tabernacle in London from 1854 until his death in 1892. "The Prince of Preachers" left a legacy that included 63 volumes of sermons, 140 books, over 60 different organizations that he helped found or lead, and a church that exceeded 4,000 people under his ministry. Spurgeon always had a passion for training young men for the ministry, especially through the Pastors' College he founded in 1857. The following quote demonstrates Spurgeon's deft understanding of pastoral ministry and especially its impact on the pastor's wife.

If I was a young woman, and was thinking of being married, I would not marry a minister, because the position of minister's wife is a very difficult one for anyone to fill. Churches do not give a married minister two salaries, one for the husband and the other for the wife; but, in many cases, they look for the services of the wife, whether they pay for them or not. The pastor's wife is expected to know everything about the church, and in another sense she is to know nothing of it; and she is equally blamed by some people whether she knows everything or nothing. Her duties consist in being *always at home* to attend to her husband and her family, and being *always out*, visiting other people, and doing all sorts of things for the whole church! Well, of course, that is impossible; she cannot be at everybody's beck and call, and she cannot expect to please everybody. Her husband cannot do *that*, and I think he is very foolish if he tries to do it; and I am certain that, as the husband cannot please everybody, neither can the wife. There will be sure to be somebody or other who will be displeased, especially if that somebody had herself half hoped to be the minister's wife! Difficulties arise continually in the best-regulated churches; and the position of the minister's wife is always a very trying one.

Still, I think that, if I was a Christian young woman, I would marry a Christian minister if I could, because there is an opportunity of doing so much good in helping him in his service for Christ. It is a great assistance to the cause of God to keep the minister himself in good order for his work. It is his wife's duty to see that he is not uncomfortable at home; for, if everything there is happy, and free from care, he can give all his thoughts to his preparation for the pulpit; and the godly woman, who thus helps her husband to preach better, is herself a preacher though she never speaks in public, and she becomes to the highest degree useful to that portion of the church of Christ which is committed to her husband's charge.

⤜⤛

C. H. Spurgeon, *Autobiography*, rev. Susannah Spurgeon and Joseph Harrald (1897–1900; repr. Carlisle, PA: Banner of Truth Trust, 1983), 443.

DEVOTION

"Apollos began to speak boldly in the synagogue, but when Priscilla and Aquila heard him, they took him aside and explained to him the way of God more accurately" (Acts 18:26).

In the book of Acts, Luke provides instructive vignettes about a married couple named Priscilla and Aquila. They had been living in Italy, but the emperor Claudius recently had expelled all the Jews from Rome—resulting in the couple fleeing to Corinth. It is unclear whether Priscilla and Aquila were followers of Jesus before encountering Paul at Corinth, but the fact that Paul sought them out implies that they probably were (Acts 18:3).

Luke describes Priscilla and Aquila as bi-vocational ministers, like Paul, supporting themselves through tent-making. While in Corinth, Paul and the couple worked alongside each other in both trade and ministry. Later, Paul brought them along and left them in Ephesus to establish a strategic beachhead for the gospel (Acts 18:18-21).

In three of Paul's letters, he mentions the couple—describing them as "fellow workers in Christ Jesus" (Rom. 16:3), as loving Christians hosting a church in their home in Ephesus (1 Cor. 16:19), and as faithful co-laborers (2 Tim. 4:19).

Modern married couples can learn several things from this ancient Christian couple:

(1) Not every couple will find the same degree of shared giftedness and calling in ministry, but it is possible for a couple to find such unity in ministry that they are always described as co-laboring together. Spurgeon is right to point out how helpful a wife can be to her husband in ministry.

(2) Interestingly, in all seven places that Priscilla and Aquila are mentioned in the New Testament, Priscilla's name is listed first. Is it possible that she was the more gifted or dynamic of the two? Apparently, her husband was not threatened to see her thrive in using her gifts. And, she even instructed Apollos, alongside her husband in the privacy of their home (Acts 18:26).

(3) Not every God-blessed ministry will produce abundant financial fruit. Whether through choice or necessity, Priscilla and Aquila worked at a trade. Modern bi-vocational ministers should rejoice that they follow in the honored path of Priscilla and Aquila.

MODERN ERA

(c. 1900–Present)

Two Stubborn Pieces of Iron

G. K. CHESTERTON (1874–1936)

As one of the foremost writers of the twentieth century, G. K. Chesterton left behind a treasury of memorable quotes. The British journalist authored one hundred books in his lifetime and contributed to over two hundred more, in addition to composing a vast collection of poems, plays, novels, and short stories. While his literary output was prolific, he is especially remembered today for his ability to capture timeless truths in pithy statements, such as the following metaphor for married couples.

Very few people ever state properly the strong argument in favour of marrying for love or against marrying for money. The argument is not that all lovers are heroes and heroines, nor is it that all dukes are profligates or all millionaires cads. The argument is this, that the differences between a man and a woman are at the best so obstinate and exasperating that they practically cannot be got over unless there is an atmosphere of exaggerated tenderness and mutual interest.

To put the matter in one metaphor, the sexes are two stubborn pieces of iron; if they are to be welded together, it must be while they are red-hot. Every woman has to find out that her husband is a selfish beast, because every man is a selfish beast by the standard of a woman. But let her find out the beast while they are both still in the story of "Beauty and the Beast." Every man has to find out that his wife is cross—that is to say, sensitive to the point of madness; for every woman is mad by the masculine standard. But let him find out that she is mad while her madness is more worth considering than anyone else's sanity.

This is not a digression. The whole value of the normal relations of man and woman lies in the fact that they first begin really to criticize each other when they first begin really to admire each other. And a good thing, too. I say, with a full sense of the responsibility of the statement, that it is better that the sexes should misunderstand each other until they marry. It is better that they should not have the knowledge until they have the reverence and the charity.

G. K. Chesterton, *The Common Man* (New York: Sheed and Ward, 1950), 142-43. Used by permission of the Royal Literary Fund.

DEVOTION

"And forgive us our debts, as we also have forgiven our debtors" (Matt. 6:12).

The model prayer which Jesus taught His disciples includes a request for forgiveness, while reminding the petitioner that he or she must extend forgiveness to others. The New Testament is full of exhortations to forgive others (e.g., Matt. 18:22; Eph. 4:32). Why? Because, in this broken world, we are constantly sinning against others and being sinned against.

Because we are selfish, impatient, defensive, and proud, when any person comes into close relationship with us, we are certain to sin against him or her. If this is true and expected in *all* human relationships, how much more should we expect it in the closest of human relationships—marriage. After all, marriage is a relationship touching the deepest parts of our emotions, sexuality, family relationships, and possessions.

Every engaged couple skipping to the wedding chapel should be required to meditate on G. K. Chesterton's words: "The differences between a man and a woman are at the best so obstinate and exasperating that they practically cannot be got over unless there is an atmosphere of exaggerated tenderness and mutual interest."

Engaged couples must acknowledge, at least cognitively, that the "perfect" person they are about to marry will soon appear "obstinate and exasperating." It is in that future crucible, by the power of God's Spirit, that they must *choose* to love and to forgive.

Immediately following the Lord's Prayer are less-quoted (though no less authoritative) words: "For if you forgive others their trespasses, your heavenly Father will also forgive you, but if you do not forgive others their trespasses, neither will your Father forgive your trespasses" (Matt. 6:14-15). If you are married, your spouse will likely trespass against you more than any other person on the planet. Are you prepared to forgive?

Sexuality and Humanity

KARL BARTH (1886–1968)

Karl Barth was known for his systematic treatment of Christian doctrine and his opposition to the German Nazi regime. The Swiss professor's thirteen-volume *magnum opus*, *Church Dogmatics* (1967), is considered among the most significant theological works in the history of Protestant Christianity. In the quote below, Barth points out a problem he saw developing in his own day that has surely only gotten worse in the years that have followed: the tendency to relegate sexuality to the merely physical realm rather than recognizing its impact on the total existence of humanity.

That God created the human being for a sexual relationship as man and wife means a call to freedom – the freedom to be both fully human and fully sexual. The physical sexuality of the human being belongs within the whole ordained pattern of being man or woman. Likewise, the consummation of the sexual relationship belongs within the whole ordained pattern of the encounter between husband and wife. All right and all wrong – and therefore also all salvation and all damnation in this matter – depend on one key question: is the sexual relation (no longer considered in theoretical abstraction) integrated inseperably into the totality of the relationship of husband and wife or is it not?

If it is not – if physical sexuality and sexual relations have their own right and power in which they may rule in some artificial zone, fulfilling only the physical appetites of the man or woman – then the sexual relations become a demonic matter. A sexuality that demands autonomy will inevitably set itself in opposition to God's command. On the contrary, when God's sovereign command confronts humans in their rebellious sexuality, their demonized relationships are "exorcised". The command of God claims the entire human being, and in so doing, it decisively sanctifies sexuality and sexual relations.

❦

Karl Barth, *Die Kirchliche Dogmatik. Die Lehre von der Schöpfung* 3.4 (Zollikon-Zürich: Evangelischer Verlag, 1951), 145-46. Interpretive reading by Mark A. Seifrid, Robert L. Plummer. and Matthew D. Haste.

DEVOTION

"And he said to him, 'You shall love the Lord your God with all your heart and with all your soul and with all your mind. This is the great and first commandment. And a second is like it: You shall love your neighbor as yourself. On these two commandments depend all the Law and the Prophets'" (Matt. 22:37-40).

To remain faithful in marriage is to obey the "double love" command of loving God and loving neighbor.

In what way?

Loving God – God has clearly revealed in His Word that marriage is to be a lifelong covenant between one man and one woman (Gen. 2:24), characterized by a love that shows the world a picture of Christ's covenantal commitment to the church (Eph. 5:21-23). Obeying God in our marriage vows shows that we genuinely love Him. Obedience is the fruit of a sincere loving relationship with Him. If we think we can arbitrarily set aside God's clearly revealed will and still love Him, we are self-deceived. The apostle John warns, "Whoever says 'I know him' but does not keep his commandments is a liar, and the truth is not in him" (1 John 2:4).

Loving neighbor – The person who loves their neighbor does no harm to them, but rather treats their neighbor as they themselves would want to be treated. What person would want their spouse to be found unfaithful in any way? Rather, we desire our spouses to be loving, sacrificial and respectful. So, in loving our closest neighbor (our spouse), we should treat him or her as we would want to be treated.

Think about your marriage anew as a place to show your love for God and a place to love your (closest) neighbor as yourself. Barth rightly points out that although many attempt to divide the sexual and spiritual aspects of life, this is an unbiblical distinction. The quote above, therefore, raises an important question: Are you fulfilling the greatest commandment with your sexuality?

Your Real Soul Mate

J. R. R. TOLKIEN (1892–1973)

J. R. R. Tolkien is best known as the author of the beloved modern classics, *The Hobbit* (1937) and *The Lord of the Rings* trilogy (1954–1955). The Oxford professor was also a devout Catholic who helped his agnostic friend C. S. Lewis (1898-1963) first understand the gospel. The excerpt below is taken from a letter to his son, Michael (1920–1984), in which he discussed the role of self-denial in marriage. It is clear that Tolkien was unwilling to minimize his own struggles for the sake of shielding his son. Rather, he pointed him to the dangers of unchecked sexual desires and provided wisdom for men and women alike who seek to pursue purity.

However, the essence of a *fallen* world is that the *best* cannot be attained by free enjoyment, or by what is called "self-realization" (usually a nice name for self-indulgence, wholly inimical to the realization of other selves); but by denial, by suffering. Faithfulness in Christian marriage entails that: great mortification. For a Christian man there is *no escape*.

Marriage may help to sanctify and direct to its proper object his sexual desires; its grace may help him in the struggle; but the struggle remains. It will not satisfy him—as hunger may be kept off by regular meals. It will offer as many difficulties to the purity proper to that state, as it provides easements. No man, however truly he loved his betrothed and bride as a young man, has lived faithful to her as a wife in mind and body without deliberate conscious exercise of the *will*, without self-denial. Too few are told that—even those brought up "in the Church." Those outside seem seldom to have heard it.

When the glamour wears off, or merely works a bit thin, they think they have made a mistake, and that the real soul-mate is still to find. The real soul-mate too often proves to be the next sexually attractive person that comes along. Someone whom they might indeed very profitably have married, if only … hence divorce, to provide the "if only." And of course they are as a rule quite right: they did make a mistake. Only a *very* wise man at the *end* of his life could make a sound judgment concerning whom, amongst the total possible chances, he ought most profitably to have married! Nearly all marriages, even happy ones, are mistakes: in the sense that most certainly (in a more perfect world, or even with a little more care in this very imperfect one) both partners might have found more suitable mates. But the "real soul-mate" is the one you are actually married to.

❧❧❧

"To Michael, March 6-8 1941," in *The Letters of J. R. R. Tolkien*, ed. Humphrey Carter (Boston: Houghton Mifflin Company, 1981), 51. Copyright © 1981 by George Allen & Unwin (Publishers) Ltd. Reprinted by permission of Houghton Mifflin Harcourt Publishing Company. All rights reserved.

DEVOTION

"Flee from sexual immorality. Every other sin a person commits is outside the body, but the sexually immoral person sins against his own body. Or do you not know that your body is a temple of the Holy Spirit within you, whom you have from God? You are not your own, for you were bought with a price. So glorify God in your body" (1 Cor. 6:18-20).

In this fallen world, our sinful nature is never fully eradicated. By a work of His Spirit, God enables us to repent and to resist temptation, but temptation remains. And, as the apostle James aptly points out, "We all stumble in many ways" (James 3:2).

Sometimes young people think that marriage will remove sexual temptation. Such is not the case! As Tolkien points out, "the struggle [for sexual purity] remains." Believers (both unmarried and married) are commanded by Paul to "flee sexual immorality" (1 Cor. 6:18). We flee sexual immorality because we recognize that God has made His people the dwelling place of His Spirit. It is completely incongruent for the holy and pure Spirit of God (living now within our physical bodies) to be brought into contact with that which God has forbidden as abominable to Him (sexual sin).

Ignoring this reality will only accelerate the consequences. Imagine that you decide to no longer pay attention to the roof of your house. Eventually, damaged shingles will result in leaks, which will result in further damage to your home and perhaps total ruin. As the author of the Proverbs put it, "A man without self-control is like a city broken into and left without walls" (Prov. 25:28).

The Scriptures teach that sexual sin in particular should not be underestimated. Again, the writer of Proverbs makes his point through a metaphor: "Can a man scoop fire into his lap without his clothes being burned? Can a man walk on hot coals without his feet being scorched?" (Prov. 6:27-28)

Have you become lax in your watchfulness over your sexual purity? Have your eyes wandered to look at things they should not? Have you been flirtatious in dress or speech? What makes you think you can scoop fire into your lap without being burned?

We Were Made for God

C. S. LEWIS (1898–1963)

C. S. Lewis was one of the most popular authors of the twentieth century. His diverse collection of writings includes children's stories, science-fiction novels, and numerous theological works, such as *The Screwtape Letters* (1942) and *Mere Christianity* (1952). Whether leading children through the magical land of Narnia or guiding skeptics to consider the claims of Christianity, Lewis was both winsome and witty. In the following passage, taken from a philosophical work called *The Four Loves* (1960), Lewis explains to his readers what will happen when they reach heaven and meet God—the One for whom we were made and the true Author of all innocent love.

We were made for God. Only by being in some respect like Him, only by being a manifestation of His beauty, loving-kindness, wisdom or goodness, has any earthly beloved excited our love. It is not that we loved them too much, but that we did not quite understand what we were loving. It is not that we shall be asked to turn from them, so dearly familiar, to a Stranger. When we see the face of God we shall know that we have always known it. He has been a party to, has made, sustained and moved moment by moment within, all our earthly experiences of innocent love. All that was true love in them was, even on earth, far more His than ours, and ours only because His.

In Heaven there will be no anguish and no duty of turning away from our earthly beloveds. First, because we shall have turned already; from the portraits to the Original, from the rivulets to the Fountain, from the creatures He made lovable to Love Himself. But secondly, because we shall find them all in Him. By loving Him more than them we shall love them more than we now do.

❧

DEVOTION

"For in the resurrection they neither marry nor are given in marriage, but are like angels in heaven" (Matt. 22:30).

In responding to the Sadducees' story about a woman married to seven brothers ("In the resurrection ... whose wife will she be?"), Jesus clarifies a teaching that is implied elsewhere in Scripture. Marriage is an institution which does not continue after death. Thus, if a wife or husband passes away, the widowed spouse is free to remarry (1 Cor. 7:39).

If a person is married to an especially difficult spouse, perhaps the chronological limits of marriage come as comforting news! But, what about those couples who can't imagine life without one another? How can heaven truly be paradise when you are no longer married to your "soul mate"?

Strikingly different from modern-day near death experiences, visions of heaven in the Bible do not focus on reunions with relatives (though such reunions are likely). The focus in heaven is on the glory and love of God. In eternity, believers will find all their needs met by God. "He will wipe away every tear from their eyes, and death shall be no more, neither shall there be mourning, nor crying, nor pain anymore, for the former things have passed away" (Rev. 21:4).

In the quote above, C. S. Lewis reminds us that all the wonderful things we experience from our spouses in this life are merely glimmers of the goodness that originates in God. When you experience such kindness and grace, don't hold greedily to the gift, but turn and give praise to the Giver (James 1:17).

Above All Consider Christ

D. MARTYN LLOYD-JONES (1899–1981)

D. Martyn Lloyd-Jones was an influential voice in British evangelicalism throughout the twentieth century. "The Doctor," as he was commonly known, left behind a successful career in medicine to enter the ministry. He pastored Westminster Chapel in London for nearly twenty-five years, where crowds of thousands came to hear his weekly sermons. He would often spend months and even years on a single book of the Bible as he progressed through the text verse-by-verse. The following excerpt is the final paragraph of his eleventh sermon on Ephesians 5:21–33, which was part of a Sunday morning series on the book that lasted nearly eight years.

Lastly, the supreme thing always is to consider our Lord Jesus Christ. If a husband and a wife are together considering Him, you need have no worry about their relationship to each other. Our human relationships and affections and loves are cemented by our common love to Him. If both are living to Him and His glory and His praise, if both have got uppermost in their minds the analogy of Christ and the church, and what He has done for the church that she might be redeemed, and that they, as individuals, might become the children of God—if they are overwhelmed by that thought and governed by it, there will be no danger of their personal relationship meeting with disaster.

The headship of the husband will be the same kind of headship as the Headship of Christ over the church. He gave Himself for her; He died for her; He nourishes and cherishes her life, He lives for her, He intercedes for her, His concern is that she may be glorious and spotless and blameless, without spot, or wrinkle, or any such thing. That is the secret—that we are ever to be looking unto Him and realizing that marriage is but a pale reflection of the relationship between Christ and His church.

So the principle of success in marriage is this: "Let this mind be in you which was also in Christ Jesus" [Phil. 2:5]. "Husbands, let everyone of you in particular so love his wife even as himself, and the wife see that she reverence her husband" [Eph. 5:33]. "Husbands, love your wives, even as Christ also loved the church, and gave Himself for it" [Eph. 5:25]. Thank God we are brought into a new life, we are given a new power, and everything is changed—"old things are passed away, behold, all things are become new" [2 Cor. 5:17]. All the relationships of life are transfigured and transformed, are elevated and uplifted, and we are enabled to live after the pattern and the example of the Son of God.

D. Martyn Lloyd-Jones, *Life in the Spirit in Marriage, Home & Work. An Exposition of Ephesians 5:18–6:9* (Grand Rapids: Baker Books, 1973), 233–34.

DEVOTION

"If anyone comes to me and does not hate his own father and mother and wife and children and brothers and sisters, yes, and even his own life, he cannot be my disciple" (Luke 14:26).

Did you know the Bible instructs you to hate your spouse? In fact, in the text above, Jesus also teaches us to hate our children, and even our own lives!

What we have in Luke 14:26 is a literal ("word for word") translation of Jesus' hyperbolic teaching in Aramaic. Just as Jesus did not intend for us to literally gouge out our eyes (Matt. 5:29) or cut off our hands (Matt. 5:30), neither did he intend for us to literally hate our spouses. It appears that Matthew has preserved for us a more dynamically-equivalent ("thought-for-thought") translation of Jesus' teaching on the same topic:

"Whoever loves father or mother more than me is not worthy of me, and whoever loves son or daughter more than me is not worthy of me. And whoever does not take his cross and follow me is not worthy of me" (Matt. 10:37 38).

The issue is ultimate loyalty and love. Only the Triune God (Father, Son, Spirit) is worthy of our ultimate loyalty and love. God is the center of all things—whether we recognize it or not. If we love anyone or anything else more than God, we are idolaters. One of the worst things for our own spouses would be marriage to an idolater! Conversely, if we follow and love God with our whole hearts, our spouses will experience as an overflow the healthiest and greatest love that can be known in married life. As D. Martyn Lloyd-Jones says so well, "Our human relationships and affections and loves are cemented by our common love to [the Lord Jesus Christ]."

Have you allowed love for your spouse to overshadow your love for God? If you are single, are you idolizing marriage or your imagined future spouse? Where is the Lord calling you to seek first His kingdom and His righteousness (Matt. 6:33)?

Your Marriage Sustains Your Love

DIETRICH BONHOEFFER (1906–1945)

Dietrich Bonhoeffer was a Lutheran theologian who lived through Adolf Hitler's rise to power. Despite the dangers, he challenged German Christians to be bold in their doctrine and sacrificial in their love for others, especially to those who were mistreated by the Nazis. Many believers today treasure his most famous work, *The Cost of Discipleship* (1937), and continue to look to Bonhoeffer as a model of courage and faithfulness. The following excerpt is taken from a wedding sermon he prepared for his niece while he was detained in a Nazi prison.

God establishes your marriage. Marriage is more than your love for one another. It has a higher worth and force, because it is God's holy institution, through which he wills to preserve humanity until the end of days. In your love, you see the two of you alone in the world. In your marriage, you are a link in the chain of the generations, which God, to his honor, allows to come and go, and which he calls to his kingdom. In your love, you see merely the heaven of your own happiness. Through marriage you are set into the world and the human community. Your love belongs to you alone as persons. Marriage is a reality that transcends persons. It is an estate, an office. Just as the crown makes the king, and not merely the will to rule, so marriage, and not merely your love for one another, makes you a couple before God and before others. Just as you first have given one another a ring, and yet now receive it once again from the hand of the minister, so your love comes from you, but marriage comes from above, from God. By the same measure that God is higher than the human being, so much higher is the holiness, the demand, and the promise of marriage than the holiness, demand, and promise of love. It is not your love that carries the marriage. Instead, from now on, marriage carries your love.

Dietrich Bonhoeffer, *Traupredigt Aus Der Zelle* (A Wedding Sermon from a Prison Cell). Translation by Mark A. Seifrid.

DEVOTION

According to Dietrich Bonhoeffer, your marriage is about more than just your love for each other. Indeed, except in cases of biological inability, marriage should result in the birth of children. God commanded the first couple, "Be fruitful and multiply and fill the earth and subdue it" (Gen. 1:28).

In emphasizing the goodness inherent in marital intimacy itself, modern Christians have often ignored the biblical and inseparable connection between marriage and the birth of children. Some Christian couples even deliberately plan not to have children.

Bearing and raising children is not easy. It exacts profound physical, financial, and emotional strain upon parents. Anyone who tells you otherwise is not giving "full disclosure"! At the same time, through these trials Christian parents discover that children are indeed "a gift from the Lord" (Ps. 127:3). We, as parents, have the profound privilege of being used by God to bring into existence a person made in the image of God with an eternal soul. We have the honor of teaching God's Word to our children, and training them to submit to authority and live in light of God's wisdom. We have the responsibility to serve, in Bonhoeffer's words, as "a link in the chain of generations." Our greatest hope for our children is that one day they stand side-by-side with us in eternity as fellow disciples of Jesus Christ. To that end we labor and pray.

In the excerpt from Bonhoeffer's wedding homily above, he speaks candidly about the goodness and obligation of married couples to bring children into the world. If a pastor had said such things at our weddings, we might have called him meddlesome. Yet, who has more biblical support? Us or Bonhoeffer?

Why Promiscuity is Wrong

FRANCIS SCHAEFFER (1912–1984)

Francis Schaeffer was a twentieth-century apologist whose ministry impacted thousands around the world. In addition to authoring over twenty books, he and his wife, Edith (1914-2013), moved to Switzerland in 1947 as missionaries, where they established a ministry known as L'Abri (French for "the shelter"). L'Abri was a unique operation that served as a refuge for spiritual seekers and a training center for young Christians. The Schaeffers sought to make everyone feel welcome at L'Abri, even as they engaged their guests with biblical truth. The following quote illustrates Schaeffer's ability to speak pastorally to the culture around him as he addresses the problem of sexual promiscuity.

In our generation people are asking why promiscuous sexual relationships are wrong. I would say that there are three reasons. (There may well be more, but in this study I want to draw attention to these three.) The first one, of course, is simply because God says so. God is the creator and the judge of the universe; his character is the law of the universe, and when he tells us a thing is wrong, it *is* wrong—if we are going to have the kind of God Scripture portrays.

Second, we must never forget that God has made us in our relationships to really fulfill that which he made us to be, and therefore a right sexual relationship is for our good as we are made. It is not to our real fulfillment to have promiscuous sexual relationships. Promiscuity tries to force man into a form which God never made him for, and in which he cannot be fulfilled.

The third is the reason we are dealing with most fully in this study: Promiscuous sexual relationships are wrong because they break the picture of what God means marriage, the relationship of man and woman, to be. Marriage is set forth to be the illustration of the relationship of God and his people, and of Christ and his church. It stands upon God's character, and God is eternally faithful to his people. We who are Christians should live every day of our lives in glad recognition of the faithfulness of God to his people, a faithfulness resting upon his character and upon his covenants, his promises.

If, therefore, the relationship of God with his people rests upon his character, and if God is faithful to his people, the sexual relationship outside of marriage breaks this parallel. Thus if we break God's illustration by such a relationship, it is a serious thing.

〰〰

Francis A. Schaeffer, *The Church Before the Watching World* (Downers Grove, IL: InterVarsity Press, 1971), 41–42.

DEVOTION

"For the lips of a forbidden woman drip honey, and her speech is smoother than oil, but in the end she is bitter as wormwood, sharp as a two-edged sword. Her feet go down to death; her steps follow the path to Sheol" (Prov. 5:3-5).

Promiscuous sex is regularly presented by secular media as exciting. If Francis Schaeffer recognized this problem in his day, the situation has only gotten worse in recent years. How much more of a threat is promiscuity to the institution of marriage when porn is never more than one click away? While such illicit sex may be alluring, the Bible warns that it inevitably results in pain, regret, and divine judgment.

Perhaps one of the most striking pictures of the dangers of promiscuous sex is that of David in 2 Samuel 11-20.

David's immoral liaison with Bathsheba resulted in an illegitimate pregnancy (2 Sam. 11:5), murder of Bathsheba's husband (2 Sam. 11:14-17), the death of a child (2 Sam. 12:14), the incestuous rape of women in David's household (2 Sam. 12:11-12; 16:21-22), insurrection (2 Sam. 12:10), and public shame (2 Sam. 16:5-8).

Unfaithfulness to your marriage cannot be kept secret. There is no hiding before the God who sees and knows all. In His Word, God teaches about the disastrous results of certain behaviors so as to keep us from being seduced down false paths. The adulterous woman does not show up on your doorstep announcing that she will destroy your family, health, and finances—but the Bible tells us that she will. Honestly pondering that truth under the empowerment of the Holy Spirit can help keep you off "the path to Sheol" (Prov. 5:5).

The Vocation of Marriage

THOMAS MERTON (1915–1968)

Although he spent over half of his life in a Trappist monastery in the hills of Kentucky, Thomas Merton was one of the most influential Roman Catholics of his generation. He authored more than sixty books; his best-selling autobiography, *The Seven Storey Mountain* (1948), continues to be popular today. Merton remained single his entire life, yet he was capable of providing a word of encouragement to couples, particularly those experiencing "the anguish of insecurity" that often accompanies the challenges of married life.

Married people, then, instead of lamenting their supposed "lack of vocation," should highly value the vocation they have actually received. They should thank God for the fact that this vocation, with all its responsibilities and hardships, is a safe and sure way to become holy without being warped or shriveled up by pious conventionalism. The married man and the mother of a Christian family, if they are faithful to their obligations, will fulfill a mission that is as great as it is consoling: that of bringing into the world and forming young souls capable of happiness and love, souls capable of sanctification and transformation in Christ. Living in close union with God the Creator and source of life, they will understand better than others the mystery of His infinite fecundity, in which it is their privilege to share. Raising children in difficult social circumstances, they will enter perhaps more deeply into the mystery of divine Providence than others who, by their vow of poverty, ought ideally to be more directly dependent on God than they, but who in fact are never made to feel the anguish of insecurity.

∽≈∾

Thomas Merton, *No Man Is an Island* (New York: Harcourt, Brace and Company, 1955), 152–53. Copyright (c) 1955 by The Abbey of Our Lady of Gethsemani and renewed 1983 by the Trustees of the Merton Legacy Trust. Reprinted by permission of Houghton Mifflin Harcourt Publishing Company. All rights reserved.

DEVOTION

"By this we know love, that he laid down his life for us, and we ought to lay down our lives for the brothers. But if anyone has the world's goods and sees his brother in need, yet closes his heart against him, how does God's love abide in him?" (1 John 3:16-17)

It's easy to imagine ourselves as great heroes of the faith. At the closing service of a missions conference, the music plays softly and we feel that we are willing to take the gospel to the darkest corners of the globe. We visualize ourselves in the shoes of Jim Elliot, dying a martyr's death and being received into glory. At the invitation of the worship leader, we stand to our feet—acknowledging our willingness to go to the ends of the earth, if so called.

Yet, as we walk out of the missions conference, we turn and exchange rude words with a family member. We fail to recognize the eternal value in fulfilling what Merton called the "vocation" of loving and serving the family God has entrusted to us.

Why is theoretical godliness so much easier than the actual task of loving the people God has placed in our lives?

The most immediate persons in need of God's love and sacrifice in your life are your spouse and children. You are the abbot of this little monastery. You are the pastor of this church. You are the host or hostess of this spiritual retreat center—charged with the physical, emotional and spiritual welfare of those under your care.

Christian, God has a plan to shape you into the image of His Son and employ you in the joyful task of extending His love visibly in this world. The primary place that love and proclamation are seen is likely in your relationship with your spouse and children. How is God calling you to sacrifice your time, comfort, or material possessions today?

After the Honeymoon

ELISABETH ELLIOT (1926–2015)

Elisabeth Elliot was perhaps best known as the widow of Jim Elliot (1927–1956), a missionary who was martyred in the jungles of Ecuador in the 1950s. Remarkably, Elisabeth and her daughter later lived with the tribe that killed her husband and helped reach them with the gospel. In the decades that followed, Elisabeth returned to America and began a career of speaking and writing. In the quote below, she speaks frankly about the realities of married life and warns of the dangers that can lie beyond the honeymoon for young couples.

A honeymooning couple may be so dazzled with love that they fail to notice peculiarities which will soon surprise them. The return from the honeymoon begins the knotty matters of the four B's: bedroom, bathroom, breakfast and budget. They may be in for a painful jolt when they find that patience must do its perfect work. He wants the windows open at night, she wants them closed. He fires his towel over the rack from the other side of the bathroom. She wants towels neatly folded to show the monograms. He shoulders his way to the mirror to shave, can't fathom how she can take such ages with her hair. Alas. What revelations begin to surface! He's used to stretching his frame diagonally across the bed, which consigns her to a triangle. But, bless his heart, the next morning he helps her make the bed—his mother told him it's easy with two. Suppose he showers and she bathes—will there be enough hot water for both? Somebody must make the coffee. Will he/she make it "right?" He expects country ham, two eggs, grits and hot biscuits, while she somehow manages on a piece of dry toast. Then, within a short time, one of them discovers that the other has no idea whatsoever about the use of money, a major setback …

A bridegroom chooses to marry a woman because he loves her. Now he must choose to *love* her because he *married* her. He ought to cherish this responsibility and thank God daily for His gift.

〜〜〜

Elisabeth Elliot, *Marriage: A Revolution and Revelation.* An unfinished, unedited, and previously unpublished draft. Available at http://www.elisabethelliot.org/Draft.pdf. Used by permission.

DEVOTION

"Therefore a man shall leave his father and his mother and hold fast to his wife, and they shall become one flesh" (Gen. 2:24).

Opposites attract. This equation is especially true in romance. The detail-oriented, bookish woman is smitten with the visionary, gregarious man. After marriage, however, the intoxication of romance begins to dissipate. Formerly fascinating differences grate upon the soul. In the quote above, Elisabeth Elliot describes these grating differences under the headings of the "four B's: bedroom, bathroom, breakfast and budget." Perhaps you can add a fifth heading from your own experience!

In the Scriptures, God commands a husband and wife to love one another and cleave to each other for life (Gen. 2:24; Mal. 2:13-16; Col. 3:18-19). Emotions rise and fall, but at the core of the marriage must be a commitment to the other regardless of circumstances or emotions. Consider the wisdom of the traditional wedding vows, in which the couple promise, "To have and to hold from this day forward, for better, for worse, for richer, for poorer, in sickness and in health, to love and to cherish, till death do us part."

If you are experiencing a portion of the "worse," "poorer," or "sickness" dimension of married life, remember that you stood before God and His people and promised to love your spouse in good *and* bad times. You likely did not realize the depth of what you were promising on your wedding day. Hardly anyone does!

The modern world thinks of love as primarily an emotion. Biblically, covenant love—the love of God towards sinners and the love of a married couple—is a love of commitment regardless of emotion.

Feelings, however, often follow deeds. If, by the power of God's Spirit, you act lovingly toward your spouse, you may be surprised to wake up one day and discover accompanying emotions. Similarly, if you act spitefully towards your spouse, you will find yourself sinking into a cesspool of negativity.

What loving deed is God calling you to now?

The Beauty of Covenant-Keeping Love

JOHN PIPER (1946–)

John Piper is one of the most recognized voices in the American church today. He was the pastor of Bethlehem Baptist Church in Minneapolis, MN for thirty-three years and has written over fifty books. His ministry has sought to bring joy to all peoples through biblical teaching and God-centered spirituality. He is best known for his emphasis on Christian Hedonism, which he summarizes in the following principle: "God is most glorified in us, when we are most satisfied in Him." The following excerpt, taken from his most substantial work on marriage, emphasizes the way individual marriages tell a story about Christ and His church.

So it is with marriage. It is a momentary gift. It may last a lifetime, or it may be snatched away on the honeymoon. Either way, it is short. It may have many bright days, or it may be covered with clouds. If we make secondary things primary, we will be embittered at the sorrows we must face. But if we set our face to make of marriage mainly what God designed it to be, no sorrows and calamities can stand in our way. Every one of them will be, not an obstacle to success, but a way to succeed. The beauty of the covenant-keeping love between Christ and his church shines brightest when nothing but Christ can sustain it.

Very soon the shadow will give way to Reality. The partial will pass into the Perfect. The foretaste will lead to the Banquet. The troubled path will end in Paradise. A hundred candle-lit evenings will come to their consummation in the marriage supper of the Lamb. And this momentary marriage will be swallowed up by Life. Christ will be all and in all. And the purpose of marriage will be complete.

To that end may God give us eyes to see what matters most in this life. May the Holy Spirit, whom he sends, make his crucified and risen Son the supreme Treasure of our lives. And may that Treasure so satisfy our souls that the root of every marriage-destroying impulse is severed. And may the marriage-watching world be captivated by the covenant-keeping love of Christ.

⋙⋘

John Piper, *This Momentary Marriage* (Wheaton, IL: Crossway, 2009), 178.

DEVOTION

"'Therefore a man shall leave his father and mother and hold fast to his wife, and the two shall become one flesh.' This mystery is profound, and I am saying that it refers to Christ and the church" (Eph. 5:31-32).

Have you ever thought of your marriage as an acted-out sermon? According to the Bible, your marriage is a declaration to the world about the relationship of Christ to His church. Your marriage is, in the words of John Piper, the "shadow" that refers to the greater "reality" of Christ and the church.

Husband, when people see your behavior towards your wife, could they conclude, "Christ is so gentle and gracious towards the church; Christ leads the church through His own sacrifice and example; Christ protects and loves His church"?

Wife, what does your behavior towards your husband announce about the church? When people see you, do they think, "The church is submissive to Christ; the church respects and follows Christ; the church loves and cherishes Christ"?

Would you ever say to your co-workers or neighbors: "Christ is harsh and unloving towards His church, and the church resents Him"? Of course not! But does your relationship with your spouse proclaim such falsehoods?

Pause and reflect: What does your marriage say about Christ and the church?

Conclusion

A few years ago, in doing genealogical research, I (Rob) acquired a copy of a single handwritten page by my great-great grandfather's brother, Rev. James Ransom Plummer, Jr. (a Methodist minister), on the eve of his wedding to Sarah Ann Elizabeth Ford. The page reads as follows:

The evening before marriage, May 8th 1851

The last night of my single life has come. Oh, with what intense interest have I looked forward to this hour! And, while many … very many … would spend this night in wild revelry and frantic glee, be it mine in sweet tranquility to hold communion with the Great and Good Being above, who has crowned my life with the highest of earthly bliss. And here would I record, in truthful words, the wondrous kindness of our Heavenly Father. He, in whose hands are the issues of life, has granted me the affections of an earthly angel, and already virtually committed to my charge, under Him, this gentle being, to protect and cherish through life's rough way. She is all I would have her to be, pure as the snow that lies unthawed upon Everest's towering summit, beautiful as the opening bloom radiant with the first kiss of summer sun and glittering with the dew drops of morning, gentle as a fondling lamb, with a mind free and untrammeled, capable of deep thoughts and investigation, pious like one who loves God and aspires to a home where angels sing and the redeemed live. Oh, how shall I be grateful enough for this loved one? And while I feel deeply the responsibility of this precious commitment, I humbly implore of Him, who all my life long has been unremitting in His kindness, that He would vouchsafe unto me wisdom and grace, that she who has plighted her faith in truthful confidence to me, may be loved and cherished through life and that together we may live, in the home of the saved, in companionship in the skies.

Written by Jas. R. Plummer the evening before he married S.A.E. Ford

Mother and Father of Martha Louetta Plummer (Mrs. B. F. Haynes)

[The last two lines are in a different style of handwriting.]

When I consider Rev. Plummer's tenderness towards his wife-to-be and his joyful commitment to purity, that legacy propels me to treat my wife with gentle and unwavering love.

Being drawn to the example of my ancestor reminded me of a newspaper article I read a few years ago. According to the article, sociological research indicates that it is beneficial for children to know their parents' and grandparents' stories of hardship. Somehow these familial stories strengthen young travelers for the trials they face in their own life journey.

If you are reading this conclusion, we assume that you have also read through the devotionals of this book. (Or, perhaps you are one of those people who reads conclusions first!) As you have considered the historical and scriptural reflections in this short volume, we hope you have received them as your own spiritual legacy. These reflections are from your fathers and mothers in the faith. They loved unto death, and you can do the same. They persevered through trial, and you can do the same. They rejoiced in tenderness over their beloved, and you can do the same. For the glory of God, empowered by His Spirit, they held marriage in honor, recognizing it as a holy institution that points to the greater reality of Christ's love for the church.

Whatever the deficiencies in yourself and your family upbringing, if you belong to Jesus, you are complete in Him. May the light of the new age of His coming kingdom shine brilliantly through you and your marriage.

Robert L. Plummer
Matthew D. Haste

Appendix

Scriptures for Memorization and Meditation

We hope the reflections in this book encourage you to go back to the Scriptures for wisdom and strength. Jesus said that a person who builds his or her life on the teaching of Jesus is like a wise man who built his house on a firm foundation. Those who neglect Jesus' teaching are like persons who build their houses on sand—to be washed away in the storms of this life (Matt. 7:24-27).

One of the best things you could do for your marriage is to memorize and meditate on the Scriptures. Perhaps you and your spouse could commit to doing this together. If you are not married, the Word of God can likewise instruct and satisfy you. A selection of recommended passages appears below.

Then the LORD God said, "It is not good that the man should be alone; I will make him a helper fit for him." Now out of the ground the LORD God had formed every beast of the field and every bird of the heavens and brought them to the man to see what he would call them. And whatever the man called every living creature, that was its name. The man gave names to all livestock and to the birds of the heavens and to every beast of the field. But for Adam there was not found a helper fit for him. So the LORD God caused a deep sleep to fall upon the man, and while he slept took one of his ribs and closed up its place with flesh. And the rib that the LORD God had taken from the man he made into a woman and brought her to the man. Then the man said, "This at last is bone of my bones and flesh of my flesh; she shall be called Woman, because she was taken out of Man." Therefore a man shall leave his father and his mother and hold fast to his wife, and they shall become one flesh. And the man and his wife were both naked and were not ashamed.

(Gen. 2:18-25 ESV)

Let your fountain be blessed, and rejoice in the wife of your youth, a lovely deer, a graceful doe. Let her breasts fill you at all times with delight; be intoxicated always in her love.

(Prov. 5:18-19 ESV)

He who finds a wife finds a good thing and obtains favor from the LORD.

(Prov. 18:22 ESV)

An excellent wife who can find? She is far more precious than jewels. The heart of her husband trusts in her, and he will have no lack of gain. She does him good, and not harm, all the days of her life.

(Prov. 31:10-12 ESV)

Didn't the LORD make you one with your wife? In body and spirit you are his. And what does he want? Godly children from your union. So guard your heart; remain loyal to the wife of your youth. "For I hate divorce!" says the LORD, the God of Israel. "To divorce your wife is to overwhelm her with cruelty," says the LORD of Heaven's Armies. "So guard your heart; do not be unfaithful to your wife."

(Mal. 2:15-16 NLT)

It was also said, "Whoever divorces his wife, let him give her a certificate of divorce." But I say to you that everyone who divorces his wife, except on the ground of sexual immorality, makes her commit adultery, and whoever marries a divorced woman commits adultery.

(Matt. 5:31-32 ESV)

But because of the temptation to sexual immorality, each man should have his own wife and each woman her own husband. The husband should give to his wife her conjugal rights, and likewise the wife to her husband. For the wife does not have authority over her own body, but the husband does. Likewise the husband does not have authority over his own body, but the wife does. Do not deprive one another, except perhaps by agreement for a limited time, that you may devote yourselves to prayer; but then come together again, so that Satan may not tempt you because of your lack of self-control.

(1 Cor. 7:2-5 esv)

Submit to one another out of reverence for Christ. Wives, submit yourselves to your own husbands as you do to the Lord. For the husband is the head of the wife as Christ is the head of the church, his body, of which he is the Savior. Now as the church submits to Christ, so also wives should submit to their husbands in everything. Husbands, love your wives, just as Christ loved the church and gave himself up for her to make her holy, cleansing her by the washing with water through the word, and to present her to himself as a radiant church, without stain or wrinkle or any other blemish, but holy and blameless. In this same way, husbands ought to love their wives as their own bodies. He who loves his wife loves himself. After all, no one ever hated their own body, but they feed and care for their body, just as Christ does the church—for we are members of his body. "For this reason a man will leave his father and mother and be united to his wife, and the two will become one flesh." This is a profound mystery—but I am talking about Christ and the church. However, each one of you also must love his wife as he loves himself, and the wife must respect her husband.

(Eph. 5:21-33 niv)

Wives, submit to your husbands, as is fitting in the Lord. Husbands, love your wives, and do not be harsh with them.

(Col. 3:18-19 esv)

I desire then that in every place the men should pray, lifting holy hands without anger or quarreling; likewise also that women should adorn themselves in respectable apparel, with modesty and self-control, not with braided hair and gold or pearls or costly attire, but with what is proper for women who profess godliness—with good works.

(1 Tim. 2:8-10 esv)

So I would have younger widows marry, bear children, manage their households, and give the adversary no occasion for slander.

(1 Tim. 5:14 ESV)

But as for you, teach what accords with sound doctrine. Older men are to be sober-minded, dignified, self-controlled, sound in faith, in love, and in steadfastness. Older women likewise are to be reverent in behavior, not slanderers or slaves to much wine. They are to teach what is good, and so train the young women to love their husbands and children, to be self-controlled, pure, working at home, kind, and submissive to their own husbands, that the word of God may not be reviled. Likewise, urge the younger men to be self-controlled.

(Titus 2:1-6 ESV)

Let marriage be held in honor among all, and let the marriage bed be undefiled, for God will judge the sexually immoral and adulterous.

(Heb. 13:4 ESV)

Likewise, wives, be subject to your own husbands, so that even if some do not obey the word, they may be won without a word by the conduct of their wives, when they see your respectful and pure conduct. Do not let your adorning be external—the braiding of hair and the putting on of gold jewelry, or the clothing you wear—but let your adorning be the hidden person of the heart with the imperishable beauty of a gentle and quiet spirit, which in God's sight is very precious. For this is how the holy women who hoped in God used to adorn themselves, by submitting to their own husbands, as Sarah obeyed Abraham, calling him lord. And you are her children, if you do good and do not fear anything that is frightening. Likewise, husbands, live with your wives in an understanding way, showing honor to the woman as the weaker vessel, since they are heirs with you of the grace of life, so that your prayers may not be hindered.

(1 Pet. 3:1-7 ESV)

TRUTHFORLIFE®

THE BIBLE-TEACHING MINISTRY OF **ALISTAIR BEGG**

The mission of Truth For Life is to teach the Bible with clarity and relevance so that unbelievers will be converted, believers will be established, and local churches will be strengthened.

Daily Program

Each day, Truth For Life distributes the Bible teaching of Alistair Begg across the U.S., in selected cities in Canada, and in several locations outside of the U.S. on over 1,700 radio outlets. To find a radio station near you, visit ***truthforlife. org/station-finder.***

Free Teaching

The daily program, and Truth For Life's entire teaching archive of over 2,000 Bible-teaching messages, can be accessed for free online and through Truth For Life's full-feature mobile app. A daily app is also available that provides direct access to the daily message and daily devotional. Download the free mobile apps at ***truthforlife.org/app*** and listen free online at ***truthforlife.org.***

At-Cost Resources

Books and full-length teaching from Alistair Begg on CD, DVD and MP3CD are available for purchase *at cost, with no mark up.* Visit ***truthforlife.org/store.***

Where To Begin?

If you're new to Truth For Life and would like to know where to begin listening and learning, find starting point suggestions at ***truthforlife.org/firststep.*** For a full list of ways to connect with Truth For Life, visit ***truthforlife.org/subscribe.***

Contact Truth For Life

P.O. Box 398000 Cleveland, Ohio 44139
phone 1 (888) 588-7884   **email** letters@truthforlife.org
 /truthforlife   @truthforlife   truthforlife.org